Remixing and Drawing

This succinct book articulates a clear framework for remixing in drawing at intermediate and advanced levels. It begins by walking through the ideas of copyright and fair use, providing context, examples, and advice. Mueller directs students through building a collection of sources and influences, leading to the development and analysis of style. With a full chapter on techniques, including approaches to brainstorming, critique, and reflection, this book features over 50 exercises that are easily adapted to various approaches, media, and technologies as necessary. Two sample syllabi are included for both a semester and a quarter system.

Ellen Mueller has exhibited nationally and internationally as an interdisciplinary artist exploring issues related to the environment, hyperactive news media, and corporate management systems. She creates experiences that engage with social and political issues through a variety of media. She is a lecturer of studio art and social practice at the University of Massachusetts Dartmouth. She previously published *Elements and Principles of 4D Art and Design* (2016).

Remixing and Drawing
Sources, Influences, Styles

Ellen Mueller

NEW YORK AND LONDON

First published 2018
by Routledge
605 Third Avenue, New York, NY 10017

and by Routledge
2 Park Square, Milton Park, Abingdon, Oxon OX14 4RN

First issued in paperback 2020

Routledge is an imprint of the Taylor & Francis Group, an informa business

Copyright © 2018 Taylor & Francis

The right of Ellen Mueller to be identified as author of this work has been asserted by her in accordance with sections 77 and 78 of the Copyright, Designs and Patents Act 1988.

All rights reserved. No part of this book may be reprinted or reproduced or utilised in any form or by any electronic, mechanical, or other means, now known or hereafter invented, including photocopying and recording, or in any information storage or retrieval system, without permission in writing from the publishers.

Trademark notice: Product or corporate names may be trademarks or registered trademarks, and are used only for identification and explanation without intent to infringe.

Library of Congress Cataloging-in-Publication Data
A catalog record for this title has been requested

ISBN 13: 978-0-367-73523-4 (pbk)
ISBN 13: 978-0-8153-9244-6 (hbk)

Typeset in Times New Roman
by codeMantra

Contents

List of Figures vii
Acknowledgements viii

1 Introduction 1

2 History and Purpose of Copyright 6

3 Fair Use 20

4 Sources and Influences 30
 Research 31
 Privilege 34
 Engaging the Senses 35

5 Style 38
 Components of an Artwork 39
  Subject 39
  Form 39
  Content 41
  Context 42

6 Copy/Synthesize/Morph 46

7 Techniques for Improving 59
 Practice 59
 Play & Brainstorming 64
 Critique/Reflection 70

Appendices: 73
A—Artist Interviews 73
B—Suggested Breakdowns of Exercises/
  Assignments/Readings 106
C—Continued Reading / Viewing List 109
D—Books and Websites for Finding
  Drawing Artists to Copy 110
E—Selected Drawing Artists for Master Copies 112

Glossary 115
Index 119

Figures

1.1	Margaret Kilgallen, *Sloe* (1999)	3
1.2	Heather Mahoney, *Untitled* (2010)	4
2.1	Justine Fox, *Untitled* (2010)	7
2.2	Originator versus Copier	15
2.3	Without This (1)	17
2.4	Without This (2)	18
3.1	Copyright Act	21
3.2	College Art Association Code of Best Practices in Fair Use in the Visual Arts	22
3.3	The markers for the various Creative Commons licenses	26
3.4	Kallie LeFave, *Needs More Chicken*	27
4.1	Five Senses	36
5.1	Ellen Mueller, *Erma Series: Leaving* (2012)	38
5.2	Drawing Media	40
5.3	Analysis Questions	40
5.4	Analysis Words	41
5.5	How an image's subject is understood will change depending on the content of the work, and vice versa	42
5.6	Critique Cheat Sheet	43
6.1	Different Types of Drawing	47
6.2	Evellin Skyers, *Untitled* (2010)	47
6.3	Options for Structuring the Term	49
6.4	Kallie LeFave, *Untitled* (2010)	51
6.5	Hadley Hansen, *Untitled* (2010)	52
6.6	Hadley Hansen, *Untitled* (2010)	53
6.7	Heather Mahoney, *Untitled* (2010)	54
6.8	Justine Fox, *Untitled* (2010)	55
6.9	Alyssa Minnick, *Untitled* (2017)	56
7.1	Exquisite Corpse	63
7.2	Hugging Lines	65
7.3	Samuel Whatley, *Thumbnails* (2012)	68
7.4	Triangle Diagram	70

Acknowledgements

This book was written in part during a three-week artist residency at PLAYA in Lake County, Oregon, which was partially funded by a West Virginia Division of Culture and History Training and Travel Grant. I also worked on the manuscript during a two-month artist residency at Bunker Projects in Pittsburgh, Pennsylvania and a one-month residency at Künstlerhaus Lukas in Ahrenshoop, Germany. Many of the images in this book were made possible by the students in my drawing courses during 2010, 2013, and 2017. Special thanks to those students in the 2017 class who gave feedback on the research copy of this book. Thank you to all of the generous artists who agreed to submit thoughtful interviews for this book. Thank you also to the reviewers of this book proposal—I know that process takes precious time and energy. Thank you to my sister, Laura Schweitz, for her many hours of reading and feedback. Thank you most of all to Phil McCollam, who spent an enormous amount of time on this project, from creating illustrations to laying out the research draft and proofing chapters. This book would not have been possible without him.

1   Introduction

Artists use drawing for a variety of reasons and motivations—telling a story, planning a project in another medium, exploring an intellectual idea, being playful, impacting viewers emotionally or physically, creating a sense of fellowship, maintaining an archive, critiquing power, creating for monetary compensation, or simply maintaining a drawing practice or routine. One motivation most artists have in common, though, is their lifelong role as students, always learning and seeking new approaches that will challenge their skills and assumptions. Keep in mind, this motivation doesn't always mean moving towards greater photo-realistic rendering skills, although that can be one approach. As artists such as April Childers or Roz Crews mention in their artist interviews (see Appendix A), good drawing can mean many different things to many different people.

Exercise 1.1 Why Do We Draw?

The artist interviews in the Appendix A of this book provide even more reasons artists draw. For example, Molly Springfield references drawing as a way of archiving, while Charles Sommer cites drawing as a means of creating new forms. Read through the interviews and find two artists that seem to draw for different reasons. Write a brief analysis of their commentary. Compare and contrast the rationale of two different artists.

Once an artist has learned the basic tools of making a drawing—such as the elements and principles of composition and practicing in a variety of media—how do they continue to move forward, to make drawings that are both interesting to oneself and others? How do they select a subject and form? How do they decide content and context?

One answer is that all artists collect and use a variety of sources, influences, and styles. For our purposes, we'll define **sources** as pieces of culture not directly related to art or design, such as—but not limited to—nature, dreams, or current events. We'll separate **influences** from sources by defining them as other artists, designers, and/or visual culture producers who stand out as impactful to the artist. This distinction is made specifically for the purpose of this text in terms of organizing research and journaling, although it can lead to some very interesting and heated debates about the flexibility or interchangeability of the two concepts. A **style** is the distinctive visual quality or the physical characteristics of an artwork. A style may be described in a variety of ways, such as tight, loose, repetitious, spilled, brushed, mechanical, colorful, quick, careful, monochromatic, faint, bold, heavy on negative space, linear, among others. Sometimes styles are associated with specific art historical periods, locations, or timelines, such as art deco, pop art, impressionism, minimalism, etc.

Students often want to develop a single personal style because their favorite artists and designers *appear* to have a single, personal, and impactful style. However, this is generally not the case. For an artist to arrive at a single seemingly unique style, they must first research, or seek out, a variety of resources and references to find inspiration and influences. Then, after (or during) their research, they draw. A lot. Artists master many drawing approaches and styles in order to arrive at one (or sometimes a few) that seems uniquely their own. As Jonathan Lethem reminds us in his 2007 article, "The Ecstasy of Influence," "Invention, it must be humbly admitted, does not consist in creating out of void but out of chaos." For example, although Picasso is known for his later abstract work, those pieces would not have been possible without his earlier works rooted in a more naturalistic style. Similarly, artist Margaret Kilgallen became well known for her distinctive style, which borrowed from sixteenth-century typograph, street art, and hand-painted signs in the San Francisco Mission District (Figure 1.1).

Artists don't create styles by trying to create styles. Artists arrive at a style through the way they approach drawing, their collected life experiences, and how those two elements intersect in sometimes unpredictable ways. Styles evolve over time through repetition and continuous work. It is a long tedious process that requires patience and perseverance. Also keep in mind, a style isn't always complex or wholly unique. Sometimes a style can emerge from the specific way an artist puts ordinary marks together.

This process of seeking out a style involves two main steps: collecting and practicing. First, artists must develop an ever-growing collection of sources and influences. Second, they must practice drawing in a variety of styles to develop a toolbox of drawing options for solving different visual problems. Therefore, **the goal of this book will be to help students execute a comprehensive survey of sources,**

Figure 1.1 Margaret Kilgallen, *Sloe* (1999) Color aquatint etching with chine collé, Somerset soft white paper, Image size 27⅜" x 17½", Paper size 36" x 24½", Edition of 30. Courtesy of Paulson Fontaine Press. Color image available at accompanying website - http://Remixing-AndDrawing.com.

influences, and styles in order to identify combinations that spark interest and create visually compelling compositions.

This book begins with a chapter which examines the history of **remixing**, or combining various works together to create something new. This chapter includes numerous examples of how copying and remixing have been central to the advancement of all kinds of ideas and creativity. It is followed by a chapter on **fair use**, which is the legal use of materials under government protection called **copyright**, as it relates to drawing. The next chapter discusses sources and influences, with an emphasis on archiving, journaling, and other reflective exercises. It is accompanied by several exercises for cultivating students' own collections of influences, such as visiting museums and galleries, watching popular art documentaries, following artists and designers both on and offline, and pursuing various research methods. The next chapter discusses style, with the following chapter introducing **the core exercise of this book, entitled Copy/Synthesize/Morph**, which results in four drawings.[1] The final chapter in the book focuses on further techniques for improving drawings through practice, play, critique, and reflection. All this study, reflection, and practice will culminate in individual presentations of sources, influences, and styles at the end of the term, giving students a chance to practice the professional skill of giving an **artist talk**, which is a formal presentation describing the artist, their art, and how and why they make their work by providing context and insight for the audience (Figure 1.2).

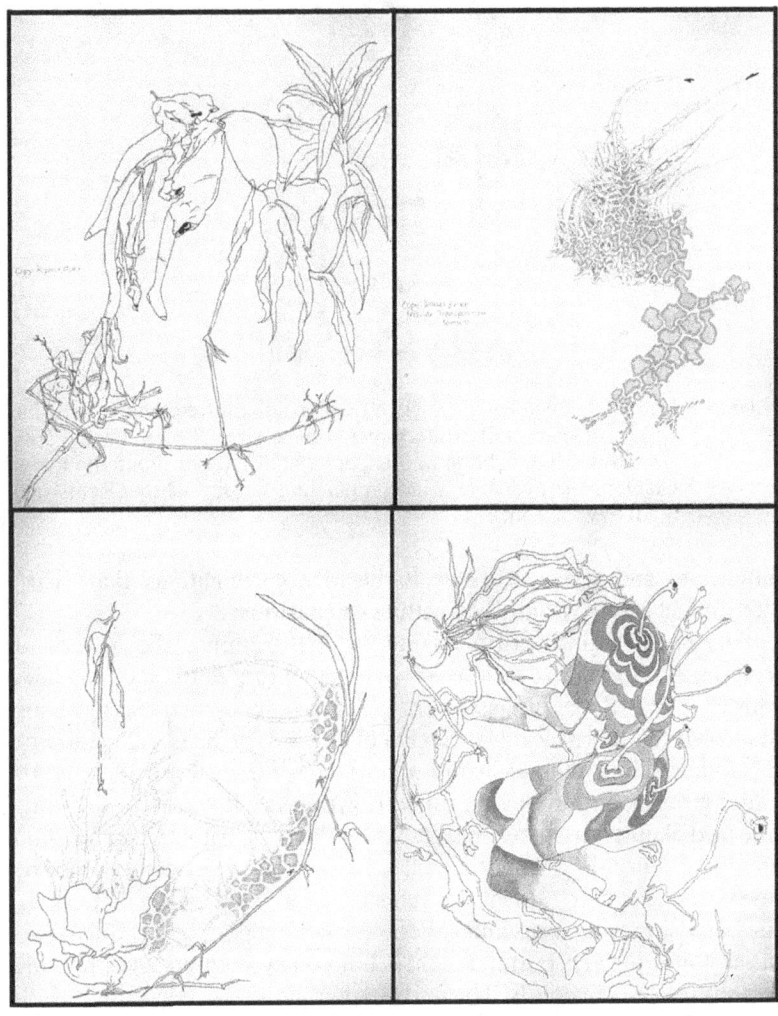

Figure 1.2 Heather Mahoney, *Untitled* (2010) Ink and colored pencil – Copy/Synthesize/Morph exercise (copying Ryoko Akoi and Daniel Zeller) for Intermediate Drawing, 4 drawings approximately 8" x 10" each. © Heather Mahoney. Color image available at accompanying website - http://RemixingAndDrawing.com

Note

1 This exercise begins by executing two master copies of two visually distinct and contrasting drawings by two different artists. The third drawing is a synthesis (combination) of the two master copies. The fourth drawing morphs the third drawing into something beyond the original two by incorporating at least one of the student's influences or sources into the composition. This exercise is repeated multiple times over the course of the term, providing an opportunity to analyze and practice several different stylistic approaches while incorporating personal sources and influences.

2 History and Purpose of Copyright

In this chapter, we will be looking at remixing and its history of moving ideas and creativity forward. Please note that although fair use and copyright are discussed as legal concepts in this chapter, this book is not a legal resource in and of itself. For further information about fair use and copyright law, please refer to the various resources referenced throughout the book and in the appendices.

Whether it is children imitating sounds as they learn their native language, or adults copying bits and pieces of pop culture as they spread memes, catch phrases, or pieces of songs, people can learn by copying. Artist Elisabeth Condon speaks on this issue in her interview (see Appendix A), making note of Chinese traditions of copying as valued learning methods, in contrast with western approaches that value originality.

It should be no surprise then that artists of all kinds, from writers and musicians to visual artists and designers, routinely **appropriate** or incorporate the work of others—either in full or in part—into their own creative work, and have done so for centuries. This process often has many different names, from sampling, remixing, and recontextualizing, to juxtaposing or recombining. Artist Guen Montgomery emphasizes the importance of remixing in her interview (see Appendix A) when she states (Figure 2.1),

> Like most artists I subconsciously borrow from the things I've seen, sometimes without realizing that I am picking up things here and there. I also remix my own work – one idea will sprout an offshoot that feels new but borrows conceptually or visually from past works.

In fact, it is very common for an artist's first pieces to be mimicry of works they admire. The **master copy**, which is the act of replicating a master work as closely as possible, has been an art school assignment for centuries. Recent advances in technology have further helped

Figure 2.1 Justine Fox, *Untitled* (2010) Charcoal and graphite, approximately 8" x 10", master copy of Frank Magnotta for Intermediate Drawing. © Justine Fox. Color image available at accompanying website - http://RemixingAndDrawing.com.

artists to borrow and incorporate the work of others, which has made remixing more commonplace now than ever.

The widespread use of remixing in the arts has developed alongside **cultural appropriation**, sometimes also known as **cultural misappropriation**, which is the process of an individual from a powerful and dominant culture adopting elements from a culture systematically oppressed by the dominant culture. Cultural appropriation involves a power imbalance, as the person doing the appropriating can profit from their creation, while the oppressed people get little or, more often, no compensation. For example, there is a long history of colonialist appropriation, where colonizers in foreign countries take a piece of folk culture—collectively created over generations—and denies local authorship while profiting from the appropriation. An example of this type of cultural appropriation often happens in relation to Native American designs, which are appropriated by non-Native American interior designers and fashion designers for profit. This form of appropriation ignores the difference in power between the privileged designers and marginalized indigenous people. Race, gender, power, globalization, and other markers of privilege and difference must always be taken into consideration when evaluating an appropriation case. Privilege is discussed in more detail in Chapter 4.

As artists, it is important to strive to avoid cultural appropriation and its power abuses. It is also important to note the terminology used here can be confusing because the word *appropriation* is a part of the phrase. In some contexts, the word *appropriation* is used to mean "borrowing" or "using without permission" without implying ties to a power imbalance. As we will discuss in our chapter on fair use, there are guidelines for using work without permission; however, cultural appropriation—where there is a power imbalance—is not acceptable. To summarize, anytime you encounter the word *appropriation*, be sure to ask yourself if a power imbalance is in place.

Certain concepts are often associated with remixing. For example, many artists use remixing to critique consumer culture, reach a wider audience, or to question the idea of originality. We can trace these critical ideas, as well as remixing throughout all forms of art, music, and writing, from the early 1900s to the present using the following timeline.

Note that while this timeline begins in 1900, remixing has been employed by artists for centuries. For example, more than 1000 years ago, the residents of Cacaxtla, a small city-state in Mexico, created a series of murals that looked very much like Maya art from 400 miles to the south. Researchers propose the artists from Cacaxtla appropriated and remixed this imagery as they interacted with traders.[1] Similarly, nineteenth-century Chinese artists appropriated and remixed imagery of partial book pages, burned paintings, and other fragments of papers in bapo, a form of painting visually similar to collage.

Timeline 2.1 Remixing, and the Tools that Made It Possible since 1900

NOTE: For a fully illustrated timeline, please visit the accompanying website: http://RemixingAndDrawing.com

1906–1919—Cubism: An art movement that purposefully ignores the traditions of perspective and naturalistic representation through a variety of tactics, including showing multiple views of a subject simultaneously. Two cubist artists, Pablo Picasso and Georges Braque, are credited with developing what we now know as **collage**, which is the act of combining a variety of materials, not just art supplies, to create compositions. An example is Picasso's *Still Life with Chair Caning* (1912).

1920s—The Jazz Age. Jazz music includes standards that are performed again and again by many different ensembles, and improvised jazz solos often navigate towards recognizable melodies, too.

1915–1924—**Dada**: An art movement focused on anti-war and anti-materialistic middle-class ideas. These artists worked in a wide variety of media from performance to poetry, photography, sculpture, and more. Dada is important to remix culture because it resulted in the **readymade**, which is a manufactured non-art object that is altered, perhaps only slightly, to reframe it as an artwork. Marcel Duchamp created some of the first readymades, his most famous being a urinal on its side, titled *Fountain* (1917). Dada also helped create the **photomontage**, which is a composite photograph made of various other photographs that have been cut and pasted to create a new composition. Hannah Höch's *Das schöne Mädchen [The Beautiful Girl]* (1920) is an example of photomontage. Dada artists Tristan Tzara and Kurt Schwitters also pioneered early **cut-up methods** by cutting the words from World War I propaganda and rearranging them by chance, rendering them nonsensical.[2]

1928—Magnetic tape was invented for recording sound by Fritz Pfleumer in Germany. This was a vital step towards remixing because it allowed for cutting and rearranging pieces of sound, whereas previous audio recording technologies, such as wax cylinders or vinyl records, were not able to be physically remixed in this way.

1930s—American folk singer Woody Guthrie appropriated common and recognizable folk melodies and changed the words to fight for workers' rights.

1935—The first audio recorder using magnetic tape, the Magnetophone K1, was debuted at the Berlin Radio Fair in August.[3] This invention allowed remixers to incorporate their own sounds, rather than being restricted to prerecorded sounds.

1940s—**Musique concrete** develops as a way of constructing music by mixing recorded sounds. Pierre Schaeffer, an engineer, radio announcer, and originator of work in this vein, created pieces such as *etude aux chemins de fer* (1948).

1942—Artist Joseph Cornell creates *Homage to the Romantic Ballet*, one of many box-based **assemblages** that built three-dimensionally upon collage traditions.

1955–1959—Robert Rauschenberg's *Monogram* is an example of the three-dimensional assemblages, also known as Combines, that built on the tradition of collage.

1959—Twenty-one years after Chester Carlson invented xerography, the first convenient office copier using xerography was unveiled, the 914 copier by Xerox. This invention would lead to the development of zine culture (pronounced /zēn/). Zines are self-published, small-circulation magazines or books that often contain original and/or appropriated text and images reproduced via photocopier. Zines often deal with controversial or niche topics that could be challenging to publish via traditional means.

1950s–1970s—**Pop Art**: An art movement focused on bringing images from pop culture and mass media into artworks in order to challenge mass consumption of everyday culture. Andy Warhol's soup cans works showcased Campbell's canned soup branding as the artwork itself. Richard Hamilton's collage, *Just What Is It That Makes Today's Homes So Different, So Appealing?* (1956) features a Tootsie Pop, a vacuum cleaner ad, and a canned ham, among other commercial imagery.

1950s–1970s—Artist Henry Darger created a massive collection of drawings and paintings using a number of collage, tracing, and copying approaches. An example of his work is *Untitled (At Jennie Richee, they admire the beauty of the tropical nimbus clouds)*, [no date].

1957–1972—**Situationism**: An art movement founded by Guy Debord and focused on critiquing capitalism. A key element of situationism was **détournement**, or the adoption of prevalent words and images from dominant culture and turning them against the system. Debord describes this concept and more in his book, *Society of the Spectacle*.

1961–1964—Beat writer William S. Burroughs adapted the Dada cut-up approach and published *The Nova Trilogy*. The first novel in this series, *The Soft Machine*, is considered his most recognized cut-up work. The Beat Generation of writers met near the end of World War II and was interested in questioning mainstream politics and culture, changing consciousness, and defying conventional writing.

1963—A group of artists in Germany—Gerhard Richter, Sigmar Polke, Wolf Vostell, and others—co-founded **Capitalist Realism**, a movement inspired by the imagery in newspapers and magazines and influenced by Pop Art in America.

1964—The first VCR for the home was released by Sony. This was a step towards allowing artists to record and view original footage for remixing outside of expensive professional recording studios.

1970—Artist Cildo Meires covertly launched his appropriation work *Insertions into Ideological Circuits* by stamping subversive messages onto banknotes and Coca-Cola bottles, then putting them back into circulation, thereby sharing his messages with people he would not otherwise reach.

1973—The first Xerox Alto computers were released non-commercially for use at various Xerox labs and some universities. This was the first computer to support an operating system based on a graphical (screen-based) user interface (GUI). Its GUI inspired Apple to develop computers that would eventually lead to the massive popularity of personal computing. Putting computers in the home helped remixing become an everyday phenomenon.

1970s—Punk Movement: A musical and cultural movement that borrowed détournement and other subversive political pranks. One of the well-known images of this movement is the Sex Pistol's *God Save the Queen* cover art from 1977.

1977—The first commercially available digital audio recorder, the Sony PCM-1, was released, making audio remixing even more accessible to artists.

1977—Curator Douglas Crimp's "Pictures" exhibition at Artists Space featuring Troy Brauntuch, Jack Goldstein, Sherrie Levine, Robert Longo, and Philip Smith focused on appropriation from photography via mass media, such as newspapers and magazines.

1978—All expression is declared copyrighted from the moment it is reduced to tangible form (ideas cannot be copyrighted)

1979—Sugarhill Gang releases "Rapper's Delight," which borrows the bass riff from Chic's "Good Times." This is one early example of remixing in hip hop music.

Early 1980s—Artist Barbara Kruger begins making her iconic collaged works that juxtapose words and photos, which question the media's construction of women as consumers and shoppers.

1980s—Culture Jamming: A term coined by Don Joyce, of the sound collage band *Negativland*, describing a tactic used to subvert or critique political and advertising messages and promote progressive change, closely related to situationism and détournement. The process critiques mass media, such as magazine advertisements or billboards, and often involves using the original medium's communication method to create satirical statements. Famous culture jammers include the Billboard Liberation Front and Adbusters.

1987—Public Enemy, a rap group known for their use of **sampling**, or including clips from other musical works which are repeated and/or rearranged, releases their debut album, *Yo! Bum Rush the Show*.

1987—Artist Mike Kelley creates one of his most well-known works *More Love Hours Than Can Ever Be Repaid and The Wages of Sin*, which consists of an assemblage of stuffed fabric toys and handmade afghans from thrift stores on canvas with dried corn and accompanied by wax candles on a table. This work remixes cast-off items to create a representation of time spent in caring for another human being.

1993—Artist Douglas Gordon creates *24 Hour Psycho*, a video work that appropriates the entire film of *Psycho* and slows it down to last 24 hours.

1993—The Yes Men, a two-person collaboration between Mike Bonanno and Andy Bichlbaum, create the Barbie Liberation Organization, which purchased Barbie and G.I. Joe toys and switched their voice boxes. They then covertly placed the toys back in stores for purchase.

1997—Artist Glenn Ligon appropriates text from a 1953 James Baldwin essay to create a series of text-based paintings entitled *Stranger in the Village*.

1998—The **Digital Millennium Copyright Act** (DMCA) was signed into law. This act stated that internet service providers were vulnerable to prosecution if they didn't take down content that copyright owners complained about, regardless of whether the work falls under the category of fair use. A counter claim can be filed, but it can take months to get content re-posted.

2004—Kanye West, now well-known for sampling and remixing in hip hop music, debuts his first album, *The College Dropout*, which pulls samples from songs such as "Mystery of Iniquity," by Lauryn Hill; "Distant Lover," by Marvin Gaye; "(Don't Worry) If There's a Hell Below, We're All Going to Go," by Curtis Mayfield; and "A House is not a Home," by Luther Vandross, among others.

2006—Artist Steve McQueen appropriates the images of British soldiers killed in the Iraq war for a work titled *Queen and Country*, which consists of sheets of unofficial postage stamps featuring this imagery.

2009—Artist Shepard Fairey is legally challenged by the Associated Press (AP) over the ownership of the original photo Fairey appropriated for his *Hope* (2008) poster. Fairey and his attorney claimed that the image was protected under fair use; the AP argued that the copyright of the photo was owned by the original photographer. A settlement was reached between Fairey and the AP in 2011.

2014—Richard Prince debuts his *New Portraits* exhibition at the Gagosian gallery in London. The exhibit consists of entirely of the Instagram photos taken by others and used without their permission. Prince's only alteration is the addition of comments beneath each picture. Multiple subjects of the photos have filed suit against Prince.

These remixing practices continue to be vital to contemporary artists in all media. As you read through the examples cited in this text, and any referenced articles and videos, be sure to return to the timeline to see what other things were happening around the same time. This sense of context can help readers to more thoroughly understand remixing's development.

Exercise 2.1 Build the Timeline

Find three more works using remixing to add to the timeline. Present images of these three works and share information on how the work utilizes remixing. As a class, compile all your timeline additions in chronological order to view how the timeline has grown.

The processes of copying, integrating, reusing, collaging, and changing is necessary for innovation, creativity, and culture to grow. Through this process of remixing, we can reinterpret and question existing works while producing new art. On some scale, all art is an act of remixing because no artist can produce new works without being influenced by their life experiences and the works—commercial, cultural, artistic, political, etc.—they have seen in the past. In fact, there are many instances of artists and other inventors arriving at similar ideas at almost the same time, despite having no contact with one another. Here is a blog devoted to such cases: http://who-wore-it-better.tumblr.com/. In some situations, one artist might be copying the other, but in many cases, the works were created without each other's knowledge.

Exercise 2.2 Three Appropriated Elements

Select a well-known drawing and identify at least three clear, visual elements that might have been appropriated. Think in terms of subject, form, content, and context.

As a reminder, the **subject** is what the artist is portraying such as people, places, and things. The **form** is the sensorial experience of the work (how does it look, sound, smell, taste, and feel), and includes the media as well as the arrangement of the compositional elements. The **content** is the meaning or impact of the work, which is created through the intersection of subject, form, and context. **Context** is the set of factors surrounding the creation and display of the work, and it can include a wide range of elements such as age, class, race, gender identity, sexual identity, geographic location, religion, culture, political affiliation, and so on.

You will likely have to do some research and may end up finding connections not only to other artists, but also to movies, books, and online sources. Report back to the class to examine the variety of approaches taken by different artists.

Often as an artist is creating, there will be intersections with imagery that falls under copyright. It is important to understand why copyright exists, and how it continues to evolve.

Thomas Jefferson considered copyright a necessary evil, in that he favored providing just enough incentive to create, and nothing more, allowing ideas to flow freely.[4] It was assumed that people other than the original creator would be able to do a better job developing upon or furthering an idea or work, thereby leading to the advancement of culture as a whole.

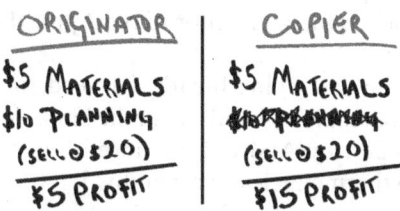

Figure 2.2 Originator versus Copier.

Thus, the original goal of US copyright law, passed in 1790, was to ensure knowledge and culture were spread and promoted. Lawmakers proposed establishing an active and diverse **public domain**, which is the collection of works *not* protected by copyright that can be used and built upon by other thinkers and creators. Originally, the law's primary beneficiary was the public, and it acknowledged the importance of copying, combining, and changing as vital to the development of a dynamic and inventive society. The law struck a deal with creators by granting them the sole rights to their work for a short amount of time—14 years, which could be renewed for fourteen more (twenty-eight in total) if the creator was still alive. These rights encouraged creation and invention by allowing creators to have a short-term monopoly on their creation, thereby profiting from their ideas long enough to cover any startup costs (Figure 2.2). This short-term profit for creators was *not* the main purpose of US copyright law. Instead, these limited profits were meant as encouragement "to promote the Progress of Science and useful Arts."

However, over time there have been alterations to copyright law to change the beneficiary from the public as a whole to the individual creator or, in many cases, large corporations and distributors. This phenomenon is practiced by some of the largest and most familiar corporations. For example, the Disney Corporation has appropriated content from a wide variety of sources to create their own animations, but have regularly fought legal battles against other artists incorporating Disney imagery into their own work, such as Dennis Oppenheim or Dan O'Neil. Disney has legally extended their copyright on Mickey Mouse—which was recently scheduled to expire in 1984—to 2023.[5] Similarly, Steve Jobs of Apple was very open about appropriating features to make his various successful products, stating in the documentary *Triumph of the Nerds*, "We have always been shameless about stealing great ideas." However, he became fiercely defensive when others appropriated from his works. In reference to Google's Android-based phones, a competitor to the Apple iPhone, he said,

> I will spend my last dying breath if I need to, and I will spend every penny of Apple's $40 billion in the bank, to right this wrong. I'm going to destroy Android, because it's a stolen product. I'm willing to go thermonuclear war on this.[6]

Through these examples, one sees **loss-aversion**, where creators feel it is ok to copy others, but not ok for others to copy what they created. This leads to a lack of acknowledgement of remixing's role in developing new works (Figures 2.3 and 2.4).

Due to loss-aversion and these profit-oriented interests, both the length and breadth of copyright has been extended. Currently, there is no registration requirement, and any creative act in tangible form is now protected by copyright, including emails, texts, or children's drawings. These changes have limited the public's ability to build on works of the past. The current term of copyright is the *life of the author plus 70 years*, or if it is a work of corporate authorship, *95 years from publication or 120 years from creation*, whichever expires first, which is significantly longer than the original term of 14–28 years. Monopolies such as these are counter to the public interest, as they limit the development of the public domain. As Lethem states, "Whether the monopolizing beneficiary is a living artist or some artist's heirs or some corporation's shareholders, the loser is the community, including living artists who might make splendid use of a healthy public domain."[7]

As the duration of copyright has expanded, so too has the concept of **intellectual property**, which implies that our culture is a market and everything of value should or can be owned by someone. Under the guise of intellectual property, Girl Scouts have been asked to pay royalties for singing songs such as "Puff the Magic Dragon" and "Over the Rainbow" around a campfire, corporations filed for patents for human gene sequences, and only since December 2015 have moviemakers been allowed to use one of the best-known songs in the world "Happy Birthday" (1893), without paying royalties. As society continues to intensify its belief in private ownership, it is the responsibility of its citizens to remain vigilant and call out attempts to disadvantage the greater good for the financial benefit of the few. This was the case with "Happy Birthday"—the lawsuit was filed in 2013 by musicians and film-makers who were billed for using the song, and two years later it was found that the music publisher did not own the song, but only some musical arrangements and therefore could not charge for its use.

WITHOUT THIS,

 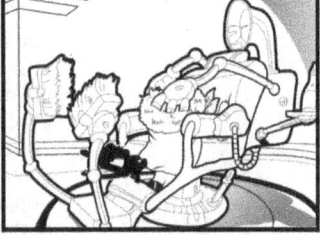

Illustration of *Modern Times*   Illustration of *Modern Inventions*

Charlie Chaplin's *Modern Times* (1926)	Disney's *Modern Inventions* (1962)
Buster Keaton's *Steamboat Bill* (1926)	Disney's *Steamboat Willie* (1928)
Snow White illustrations by Franz Jüttner (1905-1910)	Disney's *Snow White* (1937)
Pinocchio illustrations by Enrico Mazzanti (1883)	Disney's *Pinocchio* (1940)
King Kong, a movie directed by Merian C. Cooper and Ernest B. Schoedsak (1933)	Disney's *The Pet Store* (1933)
Alice in Wonderland illustrations by John Tenniel (1865)	Disney's *Alice in Wonderland* (1950)
Cinderella illustrations by Gustave Doré (1867)	Disney's *Cinderella* (1959)
Faust, a movie directed by Bertram Phillips (1923)	Disney's *Fantasia* (1960)
Fritz the Cat (1972)	*Ren & Stimpy Show* (1991-1996)
Rankin/Bass Christmas specials such as *Rudolph* (1964) and *Charlie Brown Christmas* special (1965)	*South Park* (1997-Ongoing)
The Flintstones (1960-66) and *The Honeymooners* (1955-56)	*The Simpsons* (1989-Ongoing)

Figure 2.3 Without This (1).

WE WOULDN'T HAVE THAT

Pinocchio by Enrico Mazzanti (1852-1910) [Public domain], via Wikimedia Commons

For some of the images in the chart, "Without This, We Wouldn't Have That," we can print illustrations here because they are from the public domain. However, Chaplin's *Modern Times* (1926) would have entered public domain on January 1, 2012, but due to the Millennium Copyright Act, it will not enter the public domain until 2032. Similarly, Disney's *Modern Inventions* (1962) is not scheduled to enter the public domain until 2057. Thus, these illustrations serve as stand-ins for the originals.

Examine the public domain illustrations from Franz Jüttner's *Snow White*, Enrico Mazzanti's *Pinocchio*, or John Tenniel's *Alice in Wonderland*. While Disney borrowed heavily from all of these public domain artworks to create their well-recognized movies, they have actively worked to delay their films from entering public domain themselves.

"The White Rabbit" from *Alice in Wonderland* by John Tenniel (1865) [Public domain], via Wikimedia Commons

Snow White by Franz Jüttner [Public domain], via Wikimedia Commons

Figure 2.4 Without This (2).

Of course, individual artists also rely on copyright to generate their income, which is a positive application of the law. Having work copied can be financially harmful to the original artist, as in multiple cases of large corporations stealing work from independent artists. It is important to point out that copyright makes sense for individuals over a relatively short amount of time (14–28 years), but for large corporations and artists' heirs—whose interest is in distributing rather than producing new creative goods—copyright becomes a tool of profit, rather than a tool to promote the creation and spread of new works, which was the original intent of the copyright and patent acts of 1790. This challenge is fixable; copyright is a continually renegotiated and imperfect idea. Just as it has been moved towards a more profit-centered system, it can also be steered towards embracing copyright's original goal, ensuring knowledge and culture are promoted and spread. Regardless, there are multiple ways to work within the current copyright system. Read more in the section on Fair Use and Creative Commons Licenses.

Notes

1 Allen, Susie. "Mexican Murals Reveal Art's Power," University of Chicago. Accessed August 5, 2017. www.uchicago.edu/features/mexican_murals_reveal_arts_power/.
2 McLeod, Kembrew and Rudolf Kuenzli. *Cutting Across Media: Appropriation Art, Interventionist Collage, and Copyright Law.* Duke University Press, 2011.
3 Steven Schoenherr, Steven. "The History of Magnetic Recording," Audio Engineering Society, 2002. Accessed September 30, 2016. www.aes.org/aeshc/docs/recording.technology.history/magnetic4.html.
4 Lethem, Jonathan. "The Ecstasy of Influence." *Harper's Magazine*, February 2007.
5 Schlackman, Steve. "How Mickey Mouse Keeps Changing Copyright Law," *Art Law Journal*. Accessed September 24, 2016. http://artlawjournal.com/mickey-mouse-keeps-changing-copyright-law/.
6 Jobs, Steve. "I'm going to Destroy Android, Because It's a Stolen Product." Accessed September 4, 2016. www.dailytech.com/Steve+Jobs+Im+Going+to+Destroy+Android+Because+Its+A+Stolen+Product/article23077.htm.
7 Lethem, Jonathan. "The Ecstasy of Influence." *Harper's Magazine,* February 2007.

3 Fair Use

Sometimes questions arise when remixing includes work that is under copyright. In the United States, copyright defends all types of physical artworks (as well as other things) against unapproved use. For example, you cannot make a copy of a work that is under copyright, or distribute copies of that work. You also cannot make a derivative work, such as a movie based on a book or a knock-off of a painting. You cannot publicly display, perform, or broadcast an artwork under copyright without permission from the creator. There are only two instances where the creator would not own the copyright of the work: when an individual makes a work as an employee for their employer, or if it is a work-for-hire situation, in which the creator specifically signs an agreement handing over the copyright as a part of a commission.

However, there are exceptions to copyright, which exist to ensure ideas and creativity can flourish and to preserve freedom of expression. **Fair use** is one of those exceptions to copyright protection, and it can apply to a variety of individuals, including not only artists, but also analytic writers, researchers, critics, **satirists**, documentary film makers, **parody**-makers, news reporters, teachers, museums, and memory institutions (academic libraries, art schools, museums, archives, and study centers, etc.). Section 107 of the Copyright Act outlines how fair use is determined (see the appendices for a link to the exact legal language). Keep in mind the description of copyright and fair use we are using here applies specifically to the United States, and work that is geared for a US audience. There may be different laws in other countries that affect artists who are working in other countries, or the creation of online works aimed at a specific foreign audience. See the *The Fair Use/Fair Dealing Handbook* (link in Appendix) for further information on fair use equivalents abroad. US courts generally ask four questions when determining if something is fairly used[1] (see Figure 3.1).

COPYRIGHT ACT

What is the purpose or character of the use?

Is it transformative in terms of purpose or meaning? Does this work act as a substitute for the original work? Is it commercial or nonprofit? The definitions of transformative and substitution can be interpreted differently and not all nonprofit uses will be approved. Because of this, this question will be weighed against the other questions.

What is the nature of the copyrighted work?

Was it creative, such as an artwork, song, or movie, or was it technical, such as a news story or instruction manual? Was the original copyrighted work published, or unpublished? Use of an unpublished work is less likely to be considered fair use.

What is the amount and substantiality of the portion used in relation to the copyrighted work as a whole?

Judges will examine the quantity and quality of the material used in relation to both the copyrighted work and the use, however there are no guarantees. In some cases, even using a small amount of a work can be found not fair if it is the "heart" of the work, while in other cases using an entire work has been found to be fair.

How does this use affect the potential market for, or value of, the copyrighted work?

Will the original copyright holder lose money because of this use, either now or potentially in the future?

Figure 3.1 Copyright Act.

Note that these four questions guide a court's decision-making. However, each case is considered individually by asking whether the use of the copyrighted material generates societal or creative benefits greater than the cost imposed on the person holding the original copyright. Many factors may be taken into consideration, and there is no set formula to ensure or guarantee fair use. Be wary of specific rules for remixing that are not based on the four questions US courts use (Figure 3.1). For example, some might say it is ok to use an image as long as you alter it in ten different ways, however this is an arbitrary guideline with no connection to the US Copyright Act. Instead, individually consider fair use in every artwork.

To help guide the case-by-case basis for determining fair use, the College Art Association has developed a code of best practices related to fair use, and the following four guidelines from their code are particularly helpful to artists using copyrighted material (Figure 3.2). You will notice some clear connections between the four questions posed by the Copyright Act listed previously and the guidelines listed here.

COLLEGE ART ASSOCIATION

Avoid using copyrighted material if it does not result in new artistic meaning.

If the work is sufficiently transformative, courts will often strongly favor fair use, even if the new use is commercial or includes the entirety of a copyrighted work. Be aware that simply changing the medium of the copyrighted material may not be sufficient to argue new meaning has been created. See "Is it enough?" for more.

Cite the use of others' work unless there is a specific detrimental reason not to.

Artists must be ready to explain their artistic objective.

This includes why they chose to incorporate copyrighted materials in this specific context, and what their new function is.

Artists should avoid implying that the appropriated materials are their own, unless implying this idea is vital to the concept of the new artwork.

Figure 3.2 College Art Association Code of Best Practices in Fair Use in the Visual Arts.

Fair Use 23

> **Sidebar 3.1 Conducting a Fair Use Analysis**
>
> When examining an artwork to determine if it is a fair use of appropriated material, ask the following questions:
>
> - What sort of material is being used/borrowed, and why? Is there a thorough and specific explanation?
> - How is it transformative or creating new meaning? Is it parody? Is it commentary or critique? Making an argument or expressing an opinion? Is there new visual or aesthetic meaning?
> - How much of the material is being used, and could it be as successful/transformative with less?
> - Does this new work leave a lasting effect on the original material? Could this work be substituted for the original if posted for sale?
> - Is it possible to provide attribution or credit without detracting from the new work?
>
> These questions were developed from the *CAA Code of Best Practices in Fair Use.*

Overall, it is most important that an artist can clearly describe why it was appropriate or necessary to use the copyrighted work, so judges can most easily understand whether and why the work should be considered transformative. For even more detailed accounts of how artists deal with fair use, reference the College Art Association's *Code of Best Practices in Fair Use for the Visual Arts*, which is freely available online (Sidebar 3.2).

It is also important to reiterate that not all appropriation is good, even if it is fair use. Cultural appropriation, as discussed in Chapter 2, should still be avoided. If you are unsure if you are culturally appropriating material, ask yourself what culture does this work reference, and what is my relationship to that culture? Is there a power imbalance between our cultures? Why am I using it? How accurate/respectful is it to the source?[2]

> **Sidebar 3.2 Is It Enough? Copyright and Changing Media**
>
> In Gaylord v. United States, 595 F.3d 1364 (Fed. Cir. 2010), a photographic image of a statue was chosen for a postage stamp.

In this case, the medium was changed from a three-dimensional sculpture to a two-dimensional stamp. However, the use was ruled unfair because it invaded a commercially significant market or potential market that the original artist could have profited from. If the stamp had new artistic meaning, there may have been an argument for the use as fair, but in this case the only transformation was changing the medium.

In Shepard Fairey v. Associated Press, No. 09-01123 (S.D.N.Y. 2010), artist Shepard Fairey used a photograph of President Barack Obama as a reference image when creating what came to be known as the "Hope Poster."[3] The AP, the copyright owner of the photograph, demanded compensation from Fairey because he had used the photo without permission. When looking at Fairey's "Hope Poster," most legal experts agree that his level of transformation was legally sound and did not require prior permission for use, which means the use was most likely fair. Fairey had clearly gone beyond simply changing the medium of the work. However, when Fairey was first accused of wrong-doing, he lied, denying he had used the photograph. This lie came to light and Fairey admitted he had destroyed and fabricated evidence to support his lie. The two parties ended up settling the suit out of court. Fairy's lie to a federal judge was reason enough for Fairey to opt for a settlement, even though his use was most likely fair.[4]

Exercise 3.1 One Fair, One Unfair

There are many cases of remixing that are interesting to investigate and debate using the fair use guidelines. Here are a few examples you can look up online:

- Listen to Johanna Blakley's TED talk, "Lessons from fashion's free culture" at www.ted.com/talks/johanna_blakley_lessons_from_fashion_s_free_culture
- Research and read about Richard Prince's *New Portraits* series at http://theartnewspaper.com/news/instagram-model-and-makeup-artist-sues-richard-prince-over-copyright-infringement/

- John Van Hamersveld's "The Endless Summer" poster, a 1960s design classic, appears to have been "sampled" by the Gap. Read more at www.printmag.com/article/the-felonious-summer
- Various artworks such as Marcel Duchamp *L.H.O.O.Q.*, Salvador Dali *Self Portrait as Mona Lisa*, Jeff Koons *Niagara*, Robert Rauschenberg *Ringer State (Hoarfrost edition)*, Mr. Brainwash *Sid Vicious*, Elaine Sturtevant *Warhol Licorice Marilyn*, Roger Shimomura *Liz*, Roy Lichtenstein *Drowning Girl*.
- There is an entire blog devoted to these cases: www.youthoughtwewouldntnotice.com/

Find one case that struck you as fair use, and one that does not seem like fair use. Using questions for Fair Use Analysis (Sidebar 3.1), explain your reasoning for each case.

Alternative: Select a controversial case of remixing and split the class into two teams for a debate; one team arguing for fair use, and one arguing against it. This approach is another way to practice articulating and justifying using Fair Use Analysis (Sidebar 3.1).

Exercise 3.2 Ghost in the Shell versus The Matrix

Watch the movies, *Ghost in the Shell* (1995) and *The Matrix* (1999). Write a short reflection based on these questions: What is the message of each film as they relate to remixing? Do you agree or disagree with each film's messaging? What did *The Matrix* borrow from *Ghost in the Shell*, and how does it affect your reaction to the films?

There are circumstances when artists do not need to be concerned with fair use because the work falls in the **public domain**, meaning its copyright has expired or was forfeited by the creator. A simple online search for "public domain image resources" will turn up many options for locating such imagery.

Creators may also employ a **Creative Commons license** to allow various types of reuse under certain parameters (Figure 3.3). These parameters can range from allowing others to download works and share them

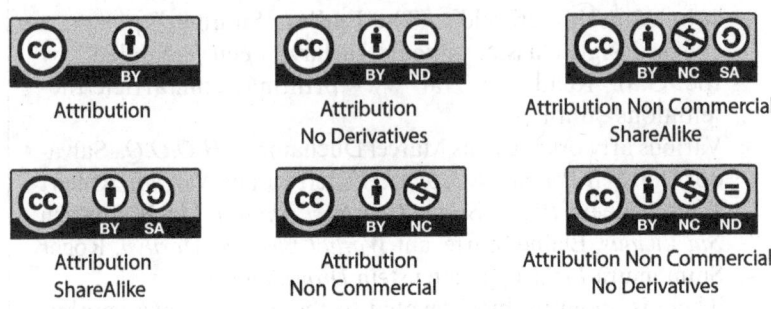

Figure 3.3 The markers for the various Creative Commons licenses.

with others if they credit the artist and do not change the work or use it commercially, to allowing others to distribute, remix, tweak, and build upon an artist's work, even commercially, if they credit the artist for the original creation. There are six different Creative Commons licenses for artists to choose from. To select a license, the artist will ask themselves questions such as, do I want to allow commercial use or not? Do I want to allow derivative works or not? Do I want people who use my work to be held to the same license terms I am using? This last question refers to an idea the Creative Commons calls **ShareAlike**; it is a way to help grow the digital commons (if an artist selects this option) by mandating further openness and sharing. Keep in mind that Creative Commons licenses do not affect fair use, which is protected by copyright law. Instead, these licenses grant a range of additional uses beyond fair use (Sidebar 3.3).

Sidebar 3.3 The Gift Economy

A Creative Commons license has connections to the idea of a **gift economy**, which is a system of exchange based on the concept of conveying goodwill or establishing a bond between people without expectation of any immediate or future reward, as in the case of ShareAlike. Other examples of the gift economy would be a stranger offering a piece of gum on an airplane, a passerby on the sidewalk smiling and saying "hello," or a person donating blood. None of these individuals expects anything in return; they are simply spreading goodwill.

Figure 3.4 Kallie LeFave, *Needs More Chicken*. Here the artist creates a piece of fan art which depicts a *Game of Thrones* character, The Hound. © Kallie LeFave. Color image available at accompanying website - http://RemixingAndDrawing.com.

A type of art that exists in the gift economy is **fan art**, or art specifically created for a community of fans of an existing body of work, oftentimes related to movies, shows, cartoons, lines of toys, and so on. (Figure 3.4) While some fan artists may attempt to profit from their work, most fan art exists solely for the appreciation of the community. Keep in mind, fan art can be challenged in court if it infringes on copyrighted materials, although some companies and creators are more supportive of fan art communities than others.

The gift economy generally exists parallel to the profit-driven market economy, aside from occasional intersections, such as the sale of art as described above. Any art that can be sold exists in both economies simultaneously because all art conveys a gift of content to the viewer, whether the viewer paid to own the work, paid to see the work in a museum, or is an unpaying viewer.

Exercise 3.3 Find and Respond

Search online to find a recent story related to copyright, appropriation, or remixing that interests you. Make sure you're checking legitimate sources: pay attention to the domain and URL, read the "About Us" section, look at the quotes (or lack thereof) in the story and who said them, keep an eye out for exaggerated language, and try reverse image searching if the illustration doesn't seem to be an accurate representation of the story. Summarize the case and your response to it providing support for your opinion.

Exercise 3.4 RIP! A Remix Manifesto

Watch *RIP! A Remix Manifesto* (available online at www.nfb.ca/film/rip_a_remix_manifesto/). What were the most important points made by the documentary? Do you agree or disagree with the film and why? What has changed since this film was made?

Exercise 3.5 Everything Is a Remix versus Steal This Film

Watch *Everything is a Remix* (available online at http://everythingisaremix.info/). Compare and contrast this documentary with *RIP! A Remix Manifesto*. Which film did you prefer and why? Watch *Steal this Film* (available online at www.youtube.com/watch?v=Ijo98_nUhrk). How does this film differ from the others? What are the dominant themes in these films?

In this chapter, we examined various guidelines for analyzing fair use, case studies of controversial fair use, creative commons licenses, and the gift economy. Now that we have this more thorough understanding of fair use, we can confidently begin employing it as artists in our own remixing works.

Notes

1. U.S. Copyright Office. Accessed August 24, 2016. www.copyright.gov/fair-use/more-info.html.
2. Cole, Nicki Lisa. "Definition of Cultural Appropriation." *ThoughtCo*. Accessed August 7, 2017. www.thoughtco.com/cultural-appropriation-definition-3026068.
3. Fisher III, William W., et al. "Reflections on the Hope Poster Case." *Harvard Journal of Law & Technology*, Volume 25, Number 2, Spring 2012. Accessed October 3, 2016. http://jolt.law.harvard.edu/articles/pdf/v25/25HarvJLTech243.pdf.
4. Cravats, David. "Despite Fraud, 'Hope' Remains for Obama Artist Shepard Fairey." *Wired Magazine*. Accessed October 3, 2016. www.wired.com/threatlevel/2009/10/faireybungle.

4 Sources and Influences

In this chapter we will define what sources and influences are, discuss ways to research and organize, examine the concept of privilege, and analyze all five senses as they relate to our sources and influences.

For our purposes of sorting and organizing our research, **sources** are pieces of culture artists collect and use as inspiration that are not directly related to art or design. Sources can include things such as news/current events, history/archives, nature/weather, memories, science/technology, literature, philosophy/spirituality, travel/place, emotions (humor, love, etc.), social justice issues, dreams, the everyday (commuting, brushing one's teeth, etc.), food/consumption, politics/power, the human body, mortality, success/failure, interpersonal relationships, conflict, geography/mapping, organizational systems, and many others. As Jonathan Lethem states, "Finding one's voice isn't just an emptying and purifying oneself of the words of others but an adopting and embracing of filiations, communities, and discourses. Inspiration could be called inhaling the memory of an act never experienced."[1]

For the purposes of this text, **influences** are different from sources because they refer specifically to other artists, designers, and/ or visual culture producers who stand out as impactful to the artist. The visual qualities of their work affect the visual qualities of your own work. It is important to study how these artists and designers arrived at their work, so you can apply similar approaches to your own work. Influences can include things such as artists (historical and contemporary), filmmakers/cinematographers, graphic designers (advertisements/marketing), web designers, architects, app/interaction designers, graffiti artists, game designers, visual culture designers (pop culture/subcultures), fashion/jewelry designers, textile designers (ornamentation/patterning), interior designers, photographers, illustrators, musicians with a strong visual presence (Lady Gaga, Beyoncé, David Bowie, etc.), and many others. You can probably immediately think of a handful of artists and designers whose work you find particularly inspirational.

Several of the artist interviews in the appendix refer to wide-ranging sources and influences. Becky Alprin has an excellent description of how other media, such as sculpture, installation, architecture, Chinese painting, and Japanese printmaking, become important sources for her drawing practice. Ian Stewart describes the importance of graffiti tags, abandoned buildings, vintage textbooks, and manual designers in his work. It is worth taking the time to read all of the artist interviews to see how the various artists' sources and influences are similar and different.

Research

Finding and identifying sources and influences is a fluid and ever-changing type of research. There might be some sources or influences that stick with an artist for life, and there are others that appear in a single drawing and then are forgotten. It is important to be open to new ideas and ways of working so that you don't inadvertently limit the possibilities of your work. One way to be open to new ideas is to research, which means seeking out what you need, whether that is new information or working to recall something you already know. You can start by reflecting on current events, topics and experiences, both personal and cultural. Identify imagery that makes multiple appearances in in your work. Try tracing and retracing important imagery. Spend time thinking about the artists you most admire and why. Ask yourself what you have in common with these artists—in terms of subject matter, biographically/contextually, visually/formally, or conceptually. Be specific in your analysis.

Always have a sketchbook or journal with you to record these important thoughts and impressions. Neil Bender's interview in the appendix details not only the way an artist can rely on their sketchbooks during the course of daily activities, but also how those casual sketches and collections of images might become important parts of other works. Also consider keeping a digital collection of these sources and influences, such as a blog. Try paying attention to the news and bookmark or print and cut out the images that most intrigue you to put into your sketchbook. Remember to make notes with the images to record why you selected them. You can also try journaling about a specific source or influence, such as dreams, the weather, a particular artist, travel, food consumption, etc. Record everything you can about your chosen sources and influences—stories, statistics, objects, feelings, etc.

Regularly go through the collected material in your sketchbook to see if there are any patterns emerging. You may notice trends in terms of subject matter, composition, and tone. It may take time for these patterns to emerge. Getting to know your own point of view, and familiarizing yourself with how it changes over time, is vital to making art that is meaningful to both yourself and those viewing your work.

The exercises below provide different approaches for maintaining an active practice of hunting out and considering new sources and influences.

Exercise 4.1 Sources around the Home

Choreographer Jonathan Burrows suggests this exercise for identifying and analyzing sources. In your home, take no more than five minutes to select one object, one book (or other piece of writing), one still image, one minute of music, and one moving image. Try not to think too much about your choices—select based on your first impulses. In your journal, for each item, write a sentence starting with, "I chose this because..." Fill in your answer by considering how the thing was made and what compelled you to choose it.

Exercise 4.2 Three Artists from a Gallery

Plan a visit to a local gallery or museum. If you are in a remote location, feel free to substitute a virtual museum tour for an in-person visit; virtual tours are easy to find online. Make it your goal to find at least three works of art that inspire you during your visit. Afterwards, research the artists to learn their biographies and previous works that may have led to the piece that inspired you. Record this information in your sketchbook.

Alternative: Visit a bookstore, music shop, novelties/sundries shop, or comic store. On your visit, record three samples of visual culture that inspire you and complete research to find out their source and how they came to be. Record this information in your sketchbook.

Exercise 4.3 Drawing You Will Not Make

At the start of class each day, watch a brief artist documentary, such as those provided by PBS's *Art:21, New York Close Up, Artist to Artist*, or *The Art Assignment*. Afterwards, take five minutes to sketch/describe **a drawing you will not make**, inspired by what you just watched. Keep in mind, since you are not going to ever make this proposed drawing, there are no restraints—you don't have to be concerned about size, media, cost, location, etc. Be ready to quickly share your idea with the class. This ongoing practice will familiarize the class with a wide variety of drawing influences and help with brainstorming practice.

Exercise 4.4 Audio Walk

Take a walk with an audio recorder (any device that records audio will work). As you're walking, react to anything that grabs your attention, even fleetingly. Make brief notes into the recorder. When you return from your walk, listen to the recording and write or sketch your observations in your sketchbook. Repeat this exercise at a different location every day for a week and see if patterns start to emerge from your observations. These patterns may reveal sources that could be important to your artistic practice.

Exercise 4.5 Paul Thek Teaching Notes

Artist Paul Thek recorded a series of diverse and freewheeling questions for students to answer in his "Teaching Notes." He created the notes for a "4-D Sculpture" class at Cooper Union taught between 1978 and 1981. Here are a few of the questions:

What do you read? How often?
What are your politics?
What do you do on a date?
What happens after death?
Are you interested in sports? Which? How often?

> Take five minutes at the start of class each day and answer five of the questions from his questionnaire. Over the course of the term, you will reflect on a wide range of sources and learn more about yourself in the process
>
> Alternative: Look up the full questionnaire online and answer all the questions (this will take a while, and you can return to finish the questions after breaks). After completing the questionnaire, report back to the class. Reflect on what your experience of taking the questionnaire was like and/or what you learned about yourself. Point out the three sources that most sparked your interest and why. In your reflection, there is no need to reveal any personal information you are uncomfortable sharing with the class or the instructor.

Privilege

As we collect our sources and influences, keep in mind, what we think and feel about them is altered by our own individual **privileges** and differences. Privileges are defined as unearned benefits or advantages we carry with us throughout life due to some aspect(s) of our identity, such as race, gender, age, sexual orientation, religion, class, etc. For example, the civil war is a source for artist Kara Walker, but as a black woman exploring race, gender, sexuality, violence, and identity in her work, she interprets this source of the civil war very differently from commercial artist Dale Gallon, a white man whose work primarily engages with more representational depictions of battlefields and other wartime scenes.

If you haven't spent much time thinking about privilege, it can be a challenging idea to grapple with. People with privilege are often so used to it that they don't immediately recognize the benefit until it's pointed out to them. When an advantage of privilege is removed or even simply revealed, people who were benefitting often feel that something unfair has occurred and may express anger, defensiveness, guilt, protectiveness, and so on. Try using the exercises below to better understand how privilege affects yourself and others. By better understanding privileges and differences, we can more descriptively and accurately describe our own sources to others. Understanding privilege also helps artists to avoid cultural appropriation, first discussed in Chapter 2.

Exercise 4.6 Two Privilege Lists

Start by folding a piece of notebook paper in half. On the left side of the paper, list all the ways you *are not* privileged, and on the right side of the paper, list all the ways you *are* privileged. This list could include things such as political association, class, geographic associations, race, mental ability, gender identity, access to technology, sexual orientation, cultural differences (values, ways of life, memes, traditions, certain behaviors, heritage), physical ability, religion, physical appearance (hair color and type, weight, height, etc.), language abilities, nationality, right-handed/left-handed, and so on. You will notice that not all forms of privilege and difference hold the same weight—for example, being left-handed does not create as many barriers as race. After making your two lists, share any findings you are comfortable sharing (do not feel compelled to share information you would rather remain private). Listening to others, you may hear things you'd like to add to your own list to make them more complete. Keep in mind all these differences as you consider the sources that influence your work.[2]

Exercise 4.7 Unpacking the Invisible Knapsack

An often-referenced and accessible article in studying privilege and difference is "White Privilege: Unpacking the Invisible Knapsack" by Peggy McIntosh. Search for this brief article online and read it. Write a short response to the reading, answering the following questions: What had you not thought about/considered before? What had you previously spent a lot of time thinking about. Share responses and discuss as a class to gain insight in the range of responses to the article.

Engaging the Senses

Another way to examine and consider our sources and influences is to engage them by using all five senses: sight, sound, smell, taste, and touch. (Figure 4.1) As you start to identify sources and influences that hold particularly strong personal significance or meaning, it is useful

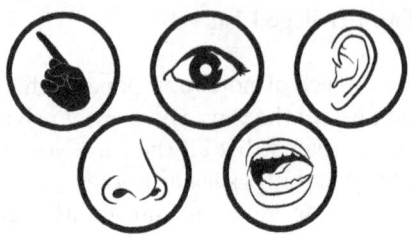

Figure 4.1 Five Senses.

to identify which of the five senses you primarily use to engage with that source or influence. For example, if you find the high desert of the western United States to be particularly inspirational, ask yourself if it is inspirational because of how it looks, sounds, tastes, smells, or feels. If you primarily respond to how it looks, take time to also thoroughly investigate the other four senses. How does it feel in the morning versus the afternoon? How does it smell when it rains? Is there any taste associated with the area? Which sounds stand out to you in the evening? By more closely examining the overall sensory experience of your chosen source or influence, you are likely to discover new ways to address this subject.

> **Exercise 4.8 Reflecting on Five Senses**
>
> Select a source or influence that interests you and write a brief reflection focused on your sensory experience of the item. Remember to incorporate all five senses. As a class, share your reflections and make alterations to your own writing as needed while you listen to your classmates' responses. Take your reflection and brainstorm ten thumbnails for possible drawings related to this source or influence. You will not be committed to executing any of these drawings—they are just thumbnails, so think big and adventurous in your quick sketches.

We collect and investigate sources and influences so we can not only create better work, but also so we can more clearly and succinctly describe our work to others. As artists, you will regularly be asked to talk about your work and your choices with individuals from a wide range of backgrounds, such as the general public, other artists, curators, critics, educators, arts administrators, and so on. Knowing and understanding your sources and influences thoroughly will allow you to help this diverse collection of people to understand your choices. In turn, you will also be better equipped to engage in discussion because you will thoroughly understand your material.

In this chapter we defined what sources and influences are, discussed ways to research and organize this information, examined the idea of privilege, and engaged with all five senses as they relate to sources and influences.

Notes

1 Lethem, Jonathan. "The Ecstasy of Influence." *Harper's Magazine*, February 2007.
2 Utt, Jamie. "How to Talk to Someone about Privilege Who Doesn't Know What That Is." Accessed September 2, 2016. http://everydayfeminism.com/2012/12/how-to-talk-to-someone-about-privilege/.

5 Style

In this chapter, we will discuss the components of an artwork as they relate to **style**, which is the distinctive visual characteristics of an artwork. It is important to be able to analyze style in order to understand what you can visually borrow from other works.

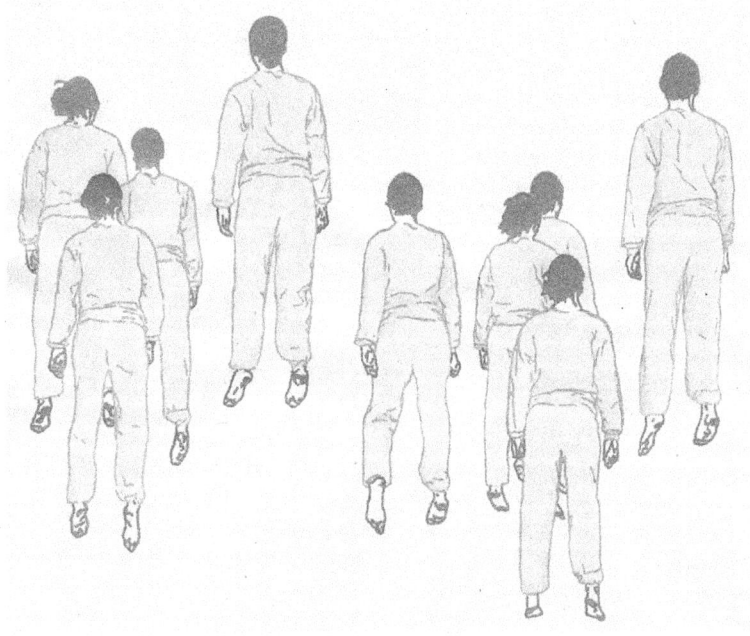

Figure 5.1 Ellen Mueller, *Erma Series: Leaving* (2012) mixed media on paper, 12" x 12". © Ellen Mueller. Color image available at accompanying website - http://RemixingAndDrawing.com.

Components of an Artwork

Subject

The components of an artwork consist of the subject, form, content, and context. The **subject** is what the artist is attempting to portray. For example, in the work *Erma Series: Leaving,* the subject is nine people with their backs to the viewer (Figure 5.1). It does not matter that the work is 12"×12" mixed media or that the image is part of a series; the subject of this image is nine people with their backs to the viewer. Typically, it is relatively easy to identify the subject in a drawing based on what we see, unless the work is abstract, in which case the subject may be conveyed using one of the other senses (sound, smell, taste, or touch). However, some works are purely **nonrepresentational**, which means that they do not depict a specific identifiable person, place, or thing. When analyzing the subject of various drawings, keep records of your observations in your sketchbook. These records can be useful when you are searching for subjects for your own drawings. When you're feeling stuck, you can simply flip through your sketchbook to stir your imagination.

Form

Form is the sensorial experience of the work (how does it look, sound, smell, taste, and feel) and includes the media as well as the arrangement of the compositional elements. When analyzing form, the first step is to identify the medium of the artwork, which could be anything from traditional materials such as graphite or charcoal, to expanded drawing media like GPS drawings, or embroidery (see Figure 5.2).

When you're examining the media used in various styles, consider starting an inventory of skills you'd like to experiment with in your sketchbook for future reference. As you select media for your drawings, think about the message you're trying to convey. Ask yourself which medium best supports that idea. Try to be critical in your choices and push yourself beyond your comfort zone.

The second step in analyzing the form of an artwork is to examine how the artist used the elements and principles of design. See Figure 5.3 for a variety of formal analysis questions and reference the critique cheat sheet (Figure 5.6) to help guide your investigation.

By examining the form in terms of the senses, media, and composition, we can start to describe the style in more detail, using descriptive

DRAWING MEDIA TO EXPERIMENT WITH

- graphite
- gel pen
- marker
- china markers
- charcoal
- colored pencil
- chalk pastel
- string
- conté
- oil pastel
- scratchboard
- spray paint
- ball point pen
- sidewalk chalk
- digital drawings
- GPS drawings
- sewing
- earthworks
- drawing machines
- pyrography
- light painting with long exposures on cameras
- silverpoint
- pen and ink
- airbrush
- leaves/twigs/other natural materials
- transparent substrates
- animation
- crochet
- cut vinyl
- staples
- glitter/rhinestones
- smoke
- erasers
- crayon

Figure 5.2 Drawing Media.

FORMAL ANALYSIS QUESTIONS

- How does positive and negative space play a role?
- Is there use of line?
- Does the work have a sense of balance?
- What shapes are present?
- How does color function in this work?
- Are there distinct textures?
- Where do you see repetition or rhythm?
- How is value used?
- Where is the viewer supposed to focus?
- What unifies this composition?
- Has the artist used scale or proportion in an interesting way?
- Where is the strongest contrast in the work?
- What is the point of view?
- Is there a sense of movement?
- How does or doesn't the artist use depth?

Figure 5.3 Analysis Questions.

words. See Figure 5.4 for a list of words that may be helpful in crafting your analysis.

As you are describing form, think about the sources and influences of the work—how did these change or affect the form? Also, think about the content or meaning of the work as it relates to form. How does the form enhance the content, and vice versa? For example, in Robyn O'Neil's vast graphite landscapes, the shimmering quality of the deepest areas of darkness enhances the fantastical concept of a place inhabited by hundreds of tiny identical men.

Context can also affect how the form is interpreted. For instance, colors, smells, and media choices can mean different things per

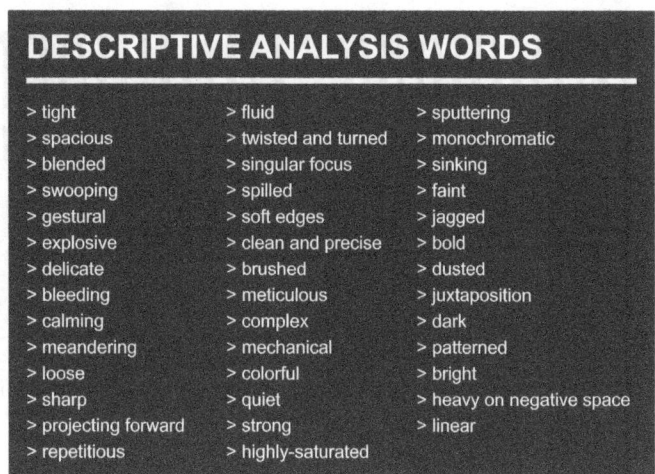

Figure 5.4 Analysis Words.

different cultural associations. In South Africa, red is associated with mourning; the section of red in the country's flag represents violence and sacrifices made during the struggle for independence. Whereas in Indian culture, red is the most powerful of all colors, holding many important meanings such as fear and fire, wealth and power, purity, fertility, seduction, love, and beauty.[1]

Content

The content, which is the meaning or impact of the work, can be emotional, narrative, sensory, philosophical, autobiographical, intellectual, and so on. Content not only affects and is affected by the form of the work, it is also affected by the subject of the work. For example, if an artist is making a drawing about the idea of "freedom," the artwork will be interpreted very differently if they are using humans or animals as the subject (Figure 5.5).

The context of the work, as the set of factors surrounding the creation and display of the work, will also affect content. For example, the meaning of a graffiti drawing can change enormously if it is shown in a gallery or on the street, as has been the case with street artists who are also engaged in the art market, such as Shepard Fairey or Banksy.

As an artist, your collection of sources and influences can be an excellent resource for developing content for your drawings. Think about the sources that mean the most to you and consider how you might

Figure 5.5 How an image's subject is understood will change depending on the content of the work, and vice versa. © Phil McCollam, http://philrules.com.

incorporate them into your work. Think about the art and design works that mean the most to you and examine how those creators conveyed meaning. Experiment with using those same approaches in your own work to see if any of them feel right to you. You can also try combining aspects of various approaches to create meaning in your own unique way. We will discuss this approach more thoroughly in the next chapter.

Context

As previously mentioned, context has an enormous amount of influence on the form and content of the work. Context includes all the external factors surrounding the creation and display of the work, including age, class, race, gender identity, sexual identity, geographic location, religion, culture, political affiliation, etc., of both the artist and the viewer/participant. These elements can all affect how the drawing is understood. Consider context in your own life—do you and a grandparent interpret art the same way? Imagine how someone from one continent might interpret an artwork created in another. What about someone of a different religion, gender, class, and so on?

An artist's sources and influences are also important aspects of context. For example, if an artist's influences are from the Byzantine era, the figures may appear very flat, and facial features may be simplified and standardized. It can be helpful for viewers to know this part of the context to better understand why the imagery looks the way it does. An example of how sources are important to context could be any well-known series, such as Monet's haystacks. If you see just one of these works, and you are unaware of how this source was used over and over to study light, you would be missing an important element of the context.

CRITIQUE CHEAT SHEET

How would you categorize this drawing? (figurative, landscape, mechanical, etc)

SUBJECT:
FORM:
MEDIA:

ELEMENTS
Line:
Shape:
Value/tone:
Texture:
Space (positive/negative):
Color:

PRINCIPLES
Balance:
Repetition/rhythm:
Focus/emphasis/dominance:
Unity/harmony:
Scale:
Proportion:
Contrast:
Movement:
Depth:
Point of view:

CONTEXT:

CONTENT:

What were the artist's sources/influences? (some research may be necessary):

Figure 5.6 Critique Cheat Sheet.

Exercise 5.1 Analyzing Style

Select a drawing artist whom you feel has a well-established style. Analyze their style in terms of subject, form, content, and context. Feel free to use the cheat sheet here (Figure 5.6).

Exercise 5.2 Analyzing Style 2

Select two artists from the interviews in Appendix A. Make sure they have different descriptions of their personal style. Write a short comparison of their descriptions. Then look up images of their work (see accompanying website—http://RemixingAndDrawing.com) and compare and contrast what you see versus what you read.

Exercise 5.3 A Style You Do Not Like

Select a drawing artist whom you feel has a well-established style and whose work you *do not enjoy*. Analyze their style in terms of subject, form, content, and context. Feel free to use the cheat sheet above. In analyzing their work closely, were you able to better appreciate the work despite not liking it, or did you find more precise reasons for disliking the work? Share with the group.

Alternative: After having analyzed the style you do not like, execute a drawing using that style. What did you learn from this exercise?

Exercise 5.4 Favorite Remixers

All of the artists interviewed in the appendix listed favorite artists that use remixing. Select two interviewees that mention the same favorite remixer(s). Compare and contrast those interviewees drawing styles. You can look up images of the interviewees' work at the accompanying website—http://RemixingAndDrawing.com.

Note

1 Briggs, Olivia. "What Colors Mean in Other Cultures." *SmarterTravel*, January 22, 2016. Accessed December 8, 2016. www.smartertravel.com/2016/01/22/what-colors-mean-in-other-cultures/

6   Copy/Synthesize/Morph

At this point, we've discussed collecting and analyzing styles. Now we're ready to practice executing styles through the central exercise of this book, which is called *Copy/Synthesize/Morph*. This exercise results in four drawings. It begins by executing two **master copies** of works by two distinctly different artists. Remember, the master copy is a well-established assignment used by artists for hundreds of years to identify the master's methods via the act of copying. The objective is to replicate the works as closely as possible, thereby pushing the student to improve skills in handling the media and understanding compositional choices. Master copying requires careful observation to determine the order of operations and robust planning in how to replicate them.

Florentine artist Cennino Cennini (1370–1440) was such a fan of master copying, he wrote about it in his book *The Craftsman's Handbook*, saying,

> You will find, if nature has granted you any imagination at all, that you will eventually acquire a style individual to yourself, and it cannot help being good; because your hand and your mind, being always accustomed to gather flowers, would ill know how to pluck thorns.

When executing master copies, it is very important to credit the work as a master copy exercise. If you fail to credit the work properly, and if the work is of very high quality, it could be mistaken for a **forgery**, which is the crime of replicating another artwork as closely as possible and attempting to pass it off as the original. This is important to remember as forgeries are not protected as fair use artworks.

When selecting two drawings to copy (and eventually synthesize), it is helpful to select two distinctly different styles. Look for striking differences in the use of line, value, form, space, color, and so on. It can also be helpful to seek out two different *types* of drawing to ensure there is adequate contrast between the two master copies (review Figure 6.1). Keep in mind, the sidebar listing types of drawing is geared toward traditional drawings, but some artists might also be interested in alternative materials, such as

Copy/Synthesize/Morph 47

DIFFERENT TYPES OF DRAWINGS

> landscape
> still life
> portraiture
> figurative art
> architectural
> botanicals
> cartoons/comics/graphic novels
> caricature
> silhouettes

> architectural/technical/engineering
> travel illustrations
> cartography (signage, maps, charts, infographics)
> food/product illustration
> animals/minerals illustration
> medical/anatomical illustration
> fiction/horror/fantasy
> collage

Figure 6.1 Different Types of Drawing.

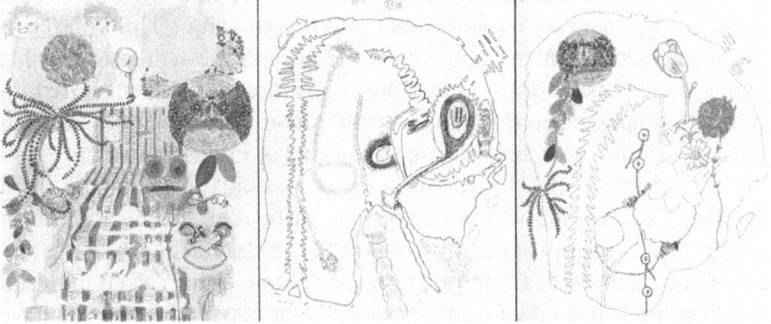

Figure 6.2 Evellin Skyers, *Untitled* (2010) 3 drawings approximately 8" x 10" each, pen and colored pencil – Copy/Synthesize exercise (copying Chris Offili and Ryoko Aoki) for Intermediate Drawing. © Evellin Skyers. Color image available at accompanying website - http://RemixingAndDrawing.com.

those that are more performative. See the artist interviews (especially Roz Crews) in Appendix A for further discussion of expanded drawing media.

It can also be helpful to seek out drawings that are executed in distinctly different media (review Figure 5.2). Finding master drawings to copy that are as different as possible will provide opportunities for interesting combinations during the third, synthesis drawing. See the appendix for a list of drawing survey books, websites, and individual artists, which can help in seeking out original works to copy.

The third drawing is a **synthesis** (combination) of the two master copies (Figure 6.2). The goal of this drawing is to intertwine the two specific styles without adding new or unrelated items (or attempting to add as little as possible). There is no single 'correct' approach to synthesizing the two drawings. The combination options are endless. Keep in mind, the synthesis drawing is still a technical exercise of replicating the master copies, but this time with a new compositional challenge added.

If you are unsure how to start the synthesis, ask yourself how you can break up the composition. What are the key components of each master copy's style? Use your analysis skills to identify the subject, form, content, and context of each style. How can the two subjects interact or fuse? What are the formal elements of each work and how can they coexist? Can you simultaneously represent the content of the two works? Are there relationships between the contexts of the works? You will want to execute several sketches to test various combinations before beginning your synthesis drawing.

The fourth drawing transforms, or **morphs**, the third drawing into something beyond the original two by incorporating one or more of your influences or sources into the composition. Spend time reviewing your collection of sources and influences in your sketchbook. What would make the most sense to incorporate into this drawing? Think in terms of subject, form, content, and context. How does the synthesis drawing make you feel? Is there anything from your sources or influences that inspires a similar emotion? Again, you will want to execute several sketches testing various approaches before you begin your fourth drawing.

Keep in mind, this fourth drawing is a departure from the third drawing. It is an opportunity to be very critical about the amount of material you are appropriating from the originals, and how well it is disguised or integrated. Depending on the volume of borrowed material and how it has been deployed, viewers may or may not notice you have sourced your choices from existing works. You have to ask yourself what your goals are with the work. Do you want this to be a statement about the original drawings, or a unique expression unto itself? This is not to say you shouldn't integrate recognizable stylistic elements into your own work, but instead to encourage you to do so thoughtfully and purposefully. Sometimes when artists integrate recognizable gestures into their work, it frees the viewer to detect other elements of deeper importance. Think about what you want the viewer to notice as you choose how to integrate the styles of the two master copies.

This exercise can be repeated multiple times over the course of the term, providing an opportunity to analyze and practice a number of different stylistic approaches while incorporating personal sources and influences. Students will find the exercise easier to execute each time. Depending on available time, students may choose to simply complete the four-drawing exercise multiple times, or some might choose to build on these exercises in a pyramid or bracket approach (see Figure 6.3).

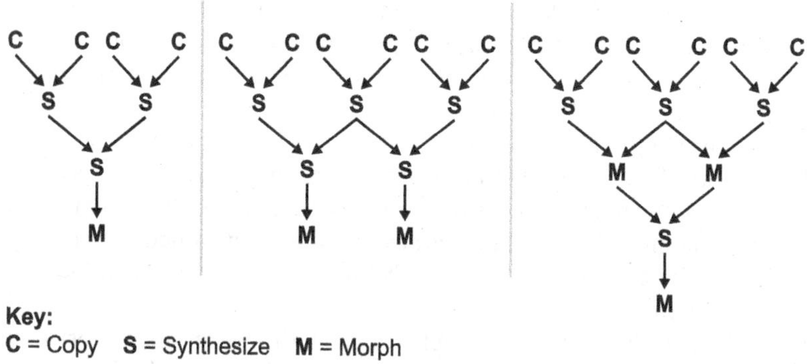

Copy/Synthesize/Morph 49

```
C   C C     C      C   C C    C C    C      C   C C    C C    C
 ↘  ↓ ↙     ↓       ↘  ↓ ↙    ↓ ↙    ↓       ↘  ↓ ↙    ↓ ↙    ↓
  S       S          S      S      S          S      S      S
   ↘     ↙            ↘    ↙                   ↘    ↙    ↙
     S                  S    S                   M    M
     ↓                  ↓    ↓                    ↘  ↙
     M                  M    M                     S
                                                   ↓
                                                   M
```

Key:
C = Copy   **S** = Synthesize   **M** = Morph

Figure 6.3 Options for Structuring the Term.

Exercise 6.1 Copy/Synthesize/Morph

Challenge: Students select two works to master copy. Next, synthesize the two works in a third drawing. Last, morph your third drawing into a fourth drawing, and incorporate your sources or influences to create something personally meaningful.

Objectives:

1 Students will be able to accurately replicate, in the correct media, two differently styled drawings.
2 Students will be able to analyze two drawings to identify and replicate key aspects of each's style as they combine these aspects into a new composition.
3 Students will be able to draw a new work inspired by the synthesis drawing and include new elements pulled from their collection of sources and influences.

Materials: Variable. Each master copy should be executed in the same media used in the original.

Strategy: Complete these drawings in the order outlined above. You will better understand the two original drawings by copying them, which will enhance your ability to combine them in the synthesis drawing. As you execute the synthesis, think about how your sources and influences relate to this new composition, and can be added to the morph drawing.

Key Questions: What are the most important techniques involved in imitating these drawings? What are the key elements of each drawing's style? Think in terms of the elements and principles of design. What makes a good composition?

Critiquing Strategy: Work in pairs to critique works after each stage of the exercise. Do not start executing the synthesis drawing until the master copies have been critiqued. Similarly, do not start the morph until the synthesis has been critiqued. Review the feedback from the pairs with the full class to see if others agree with the critique.

Timetable: A week for each stage of the assignment works well: one week for master copies, one week for synthesis, one week for morph.

Alternative Copy/Synthesize/Morph Exercise #1

See what happens when you try to execute the Copy/Synthesize/Morph exercise using one alternative-media drawing and one more traditional-media drawing as your master copies. Alternative drawing media could be string or thread, as in Gabriel Dawe's "Plexus A1" (2015). Richard Long made performance-based drawings using walking to create lines in the landscape, such as "Walking a Line in Peru" (1972). Cai Guo-Qiang uses gunpowder to create drawings, and Brian Hart uses flashlights and long photographic exposures to create drawings with light. Spend some time researching before you settle on an alternative-media drawing to master copy.

Alternative Copy/Synthesize/Morph Exercise #2

See what happens when you add an additional constraint to your morph drawing. For example, what happens when your Morph drawing is at a completely different scale than your copies and synthesis works? What happens if you switch media for the morph drawing—for example, if your master copies were in graphite and pen, what happens when you change the media to gesso and charcoal, or even more different—such as animation—for the morph drawing? (Figures 6.4 – 6.9).

Figure 6.4 Kallie LeFave, *Untitled* (2010) Acrylic, conte, marker, and ink – Copy/Synthesize/Morph exercise (copying Deuce7 and Leonardo DaVinci) for Intermediate Drawing, 4 drawings approximately 8" x 10" each. © Kallie LeFave. Color image available at accompanying website - http://RemixingAndDrawing.com.

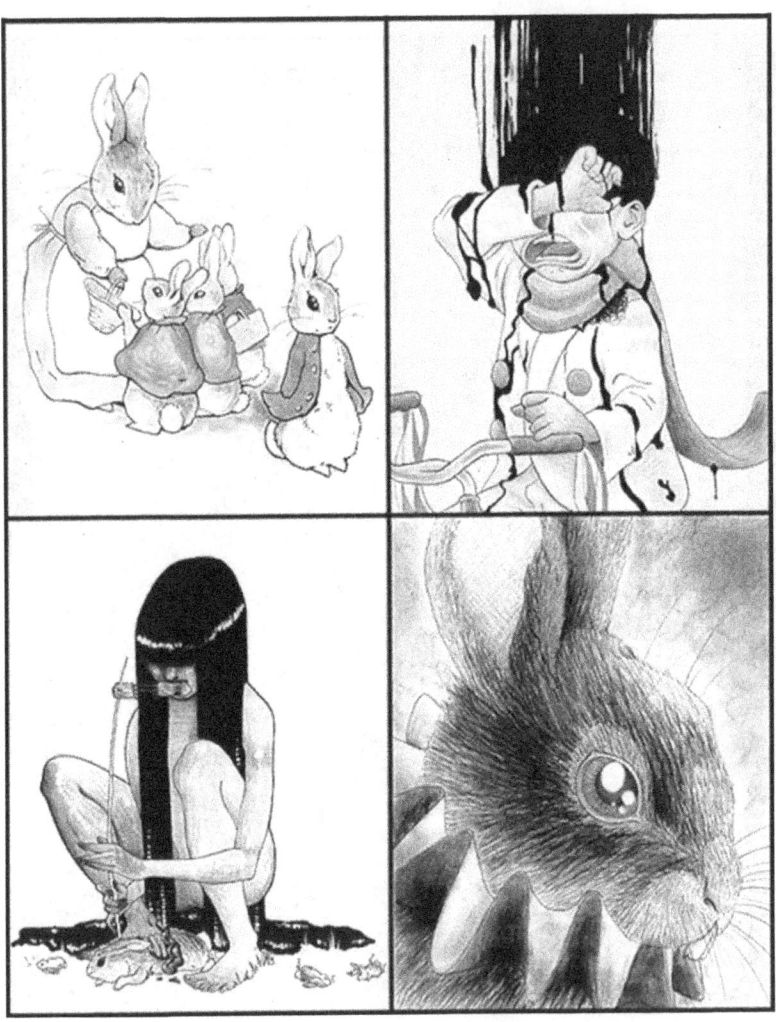

Figure 6.5 Hadley Hansen, *Untitled* (2010) Ink and colored pencil – Copy/Synthesize/Morph exercise (copying Beatrix Potter and James Jean) for Intermediate Drawing, 4 drawings approx. 10" x 8" each. © Hadley Hansen. Color image available at accompanying website - http://RemixingAndDrawing.com.

Figure 6.6 Hadley Hansen, *Untitled* (2010) mixed media on paper, 4 drawings approx. 10" x 8" each. Copy/Synthesize/Morph exercise (copying Tim Burton and Zak Smith) for Intermediate Drawing. © Hadley Hansen. Color image available at accompanying website - http://RemixingAndDrawing.com.

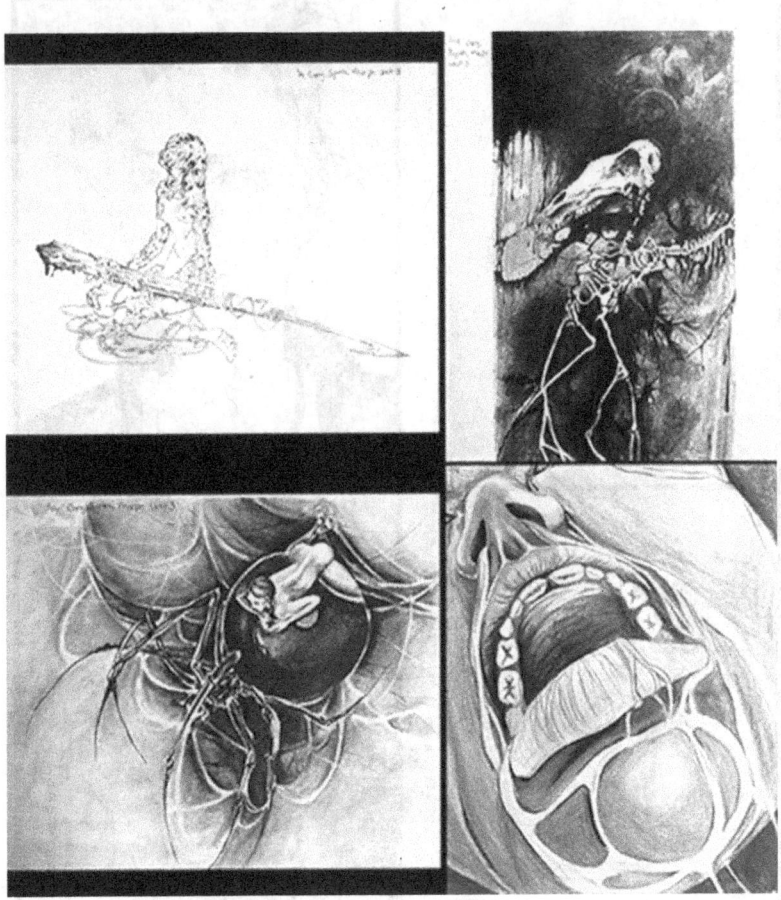

Figure 6.7 Heather Mahoney, *Untitled* (2010) mixed media on paper, 4 drawings approx. 10" x 8" each. Copy/Synthesize/Morph exercise (copying James Jean and Stephen Gammell) for Intermediate Drawing. © Heather Mahoney. Color image available at accompanying website - http://RemixingAndDrawing.com.

Figure 6.8 Justine Fox, *Untitled* (2010) mixed media on paper, 4 drawings approx. 10" x 8" each. Copy/Synthesize/Morph exercise (copying Graham Little and Pavel Pepperstein) for Intermediate Drawing. © Justine Fox. Color image available at accompanying website - http://RemixingAndDrawing.com.

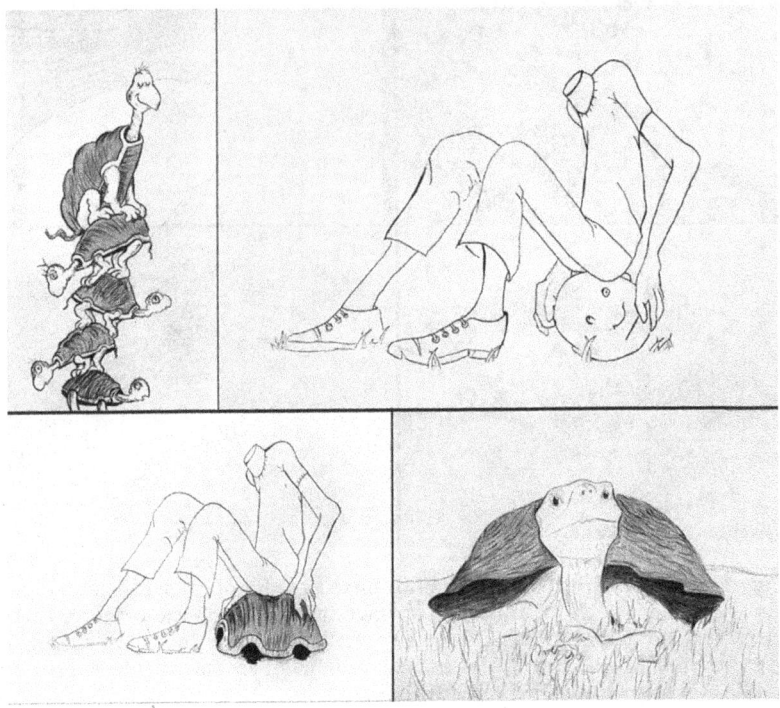

Figure 6.9 Alyssa Minnick, *Untitled* (2017) mixed media on paper, 4 drawings varying sizes. Copy/Synthesize/Morph exercise (copying Dr. Seuss and Shell Silverstein) for Intermediate Drawing. © Alyssa Minnick. Color image available at accompanying website - http://RemixingAndDrawing.com

Exercise 6.2 Synthesis Practice

For this exercise, you will synthesize two drawings. Then, you will write down directions, also known as a **score**, for completing the series of tasks necessary to synthesize two drawings. Possibly the most famous drawing artist using scores is Sol Lewitt. He believed that, similar to an architect producing blueprints for buildings and then giving the plans to a construction crew, "an artist should be able to conceive of a work and then either delegate its actual production to others or perhaps even never make it at all."[1] Your task is to write a score for this synthesis drawing. Give the score to someone else to execute. Compare your drawings to their drawings based on the score.

Exercise 6.3 Artist Talk

Challenge: Students will prepare a short artist talk—no more than five to ten minutes—describing sources, influences, and preferred style(s).

Objectives:

1 Students will demonstrate excellent public speaking skills (volume, physical appearance, pacing, organization, preparation).
2 Students will demonstrate storytelling skills by using an introduction, conclusion, and personal anecdotes.
3 Students will be detailed and specific in their descriptions of sources, influences, and styles.
4 Students will develop effective communication tools (presentation images/props) that stir the curiosity of the audience.

Materials: The form of the presentation can be flexible. The most common approach might be an on-screen slide show, but you might also consider bringing in props to illustrate your style(s). Some might develop a poster or book to accompany the talk.

Strategy: Begin your presentation with your sources and influences. This information should be easy to locate in your sketchbook based on all the research and analysis you have completed over the term. Remember, your audience will want to know what made you interested in these sources and influences in the first place—tell a story. What appears obvious to you might not be obvious to others. Next, describe your style, and use images of your work to illustrate your points. Be sure to discuss aspects of privilege and address the five senses as necessary. These are important details that shouldn't be left out. As you near the end of your presentation, mention what you are currently working on, or what you plan on working on next. At this point, it's ok to mention things you are reading, looking at, thinking about, and doing that may or may not impact your future drawing practice. Audiences can identify with that uncertainty and will also appreciate your honesty.

Key Questions: Have you told a story about what you make and why? Have you been detailed and specific about your sources, influences, and style(s)? Have you mentioned what you are presently working on or future projects?

Critiquing Strategy: Do an in-progress critique with small groups and a final critique with the full class. The in-progress critique allows students to listen to others' artist talks, observe successes, and alter their own talks accordingly.

Timetable: Artist talks work best when presented at the end of the term, allowing students maximum time to think about their sources and influences. Allow at least one week for students to develop a first draft of the presentation for small-group critique. Allow additional out-of-class time after the first critique for students to make improvements before performing the artist talk to the entire class for a grade.

Note

1 The Art Story: Modern Art Insight. Internet. Accessed May 14, 2017. www.theartstory.org/artist-lewitt-sol.htm

7 Techniques for Improving

Copy/Synthesize/Morph is one exercise that has been proven to be an excellent tool for improving drawing skills, but it certainly isn't the only one. Maintaining a sense of variety in your drawing practice is crucial to continued improvement. Also, making sure to maintain your sense of play and self-reflection will ensure you continue to grow and improve as an artist. This chapter aims to provide a wide array of exercises to add diversification to your practice, cultivate a sense of play, and provide ways to critique and reflect on your work as you continue to grow and learn as a drawing artist.

Practice

Practice, on a regular basis, is key to improving your drawings. Having a large collection of different drawing challenges, exercises, or prompts is vital to growing as an artist. Establish a daily drawing practice or ritual. Schedule your drawing time each day and commit to that time. It doesn't have to be a long time—20 or 30 minutes is fine. Often, you will find that once you start drawing, you will want to continue beyond your allotted time. Since one of the biggest challenges is getting started, it can be helpful to schedule drawing time the same way you would any other appointment. If possible, it's also helpful to try to keep your drawing time at the same time every day. This will help establish a habit. However, if you cannot find the same time every day, it is ok to place that drawing block at any time that works for your schedule.

Timing your drawings is a great way to set boundaries within which you can work and against which you can react. The amount of time can be flexible to meet your needs and fit your schedule. Experiment with different amounts of time and try to identify the amount of time that is most productive for you. If you are struggling to think of what to draw, you can consult a book of prompts, such as Chronicle Book's series: *642 Things to Draw, 642 Tiny Things to Draw, 712 More Things to Draw, 642 Big Things to Draw, 642 Fashion Things to Draw*, etc., or use any number of online drawing prompt generators, such as http://artprompts.org.

Exercise 7.1 Visual Language

Several of the artists in the interviews (see Appendix) mention the development of a visual language. For example, Julia Oldham mentions how her animations have a specific visual language in comparison with the photographs she uses in her work. Take a moment to think about your own visual language. What would be your nouns, verbs, adverbs, and adjectives? Can you create a visual dictionary for your visual language? Try doing this exercise once a month, and ask yourself how your visual language has developed and changed over time.

Exercise 7.2 Daily Portraits

Daily portraits can be a great way to improve your skills in observing and rendering proportions. In a classroom setting, you can work in pairs, executing portraits of your classmates every day. You can draw your classmate as they draw you. You might also choose a specific amount of time you will dedicate to these portraits each day. If you are working outside of a class, you can go to a public place (a library, coffee shop, etc.) and draw a portrait of someone in that space. As you complete more portraits, in can be helpful to introduce new challenges, such as working in a variety of media. You could select a new media each week or month.

Alternative

You could draw a daily self-portrait if you don't want to draw others. Challenge yourself to never draw the same self-portrait in terms of pose, color, or media.

Exercise 7.3 Pick a Room

Pick a room in the place you live. Each day draw one object from the room until you have drawn every element of the room. Use this exercise to practice observational drawing on a daily basis.

Exercise 7.4 Popcorn

Make a bowl of popcorn without any toppings. Each day, draw one kernel of popcorn. Throw away the kernel when you are finished. Continue this practice until you have used up the entire bowl of popcorn. Drawing popcorn requires an attention to detail and value, which is a great way to strengthen your observational drawing skills. In these drawings, feel free to use any media, substrate [paper, board, etc.], and scale you like.

Exercise 7.5 Mapping

Each day, draw a map. It could be a map of a place you know, an imagined place, or a real location you've never been to. It could be a walking, driving, flying, riding, biking, or skating map (insert any mode of transportation you like). It could be a map explaining how to navigate systems that are unrelated to transportation (how to get through college or high school, how to select a movie, how to discuss a challenging topic with a stranger, etc.). Challenge yourself to communicate with as few words as possible. Think about what symbols and objects could most clearly communicate the purpose of the map.

Exercise 7.6 Multiday Drawings

Make three- or five-day drawings. Start by drawing one object on a piece of paper, then, on the next day, draw another subject on top of the first one; repeat this process for three to five days. Pay attention to how and where the subjects overlap—where are the overhangs? Are they nearly perfectly overlapping, or hardly at all? What happens when you do this exercise all in one color? What happens when you use a monochromatic color scheme? What happens when you use a more complex color scheme? You can experiment with scale, media, color, processes, viewpoints, etc.

Exercise 7.7 Holiday Sales

Another daily drawing challenge can align with various holidays. www.holidayinsights.com has an extensive list of holidays and historical events to inspire a daily drawing practice. As you complete your daily drawing, you can photograph, scan, or trace the work by hand or using software. Then, upload the work to an online shop (such as Etsy, Big Cartel, etc.) or a print-on-demand shop (RedBubble, Threadless, Society6, Zazzle, etc.). This can be an opportunity to learn about professional practices: managing prices, tracking sales, promoting, etc.

Exercise 7.8 Location Exploration

Each day, go to a new location. Give yourself a time limit, and explore this new location through drawing. You might even make a small map to accompany your drawing. This exercise can help challenge your drawing practice by adding the unfamiliar.

Exercise 7.9 Exquisite Corpse

Engage in an exquisite corpse collaboration with other artists. In a classroom setting, this is fairly easy: everyone draws a partial drawing and then covers it up with a piece of paper, except for a tiny clue for the next person to continue the drawing. Do one section of drawing each day, passing each person's exquisite corpse to the next person until the paper is full (Figure 7.1).

Techniques for Improving 63

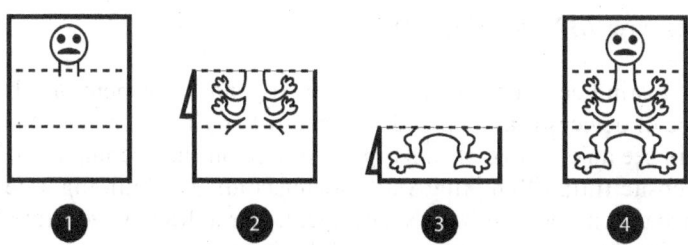

Figure 7.1 Exquisite Corpse.

Alternative

If you are not in a classroom, you can do the same thing with artists far away from you. Complete the first step by creating a partial drawing and then covering it up with paper, except for a tiny clue for the next artist. Mail that drawing to an artist. Each day, complete this first step and mail it to a different artist (keep in mind, you should contact the artist first to ensure they want to participate). Continue this process and encourage the other artists in your group to also send you their exquisite corpses to build upon.

Exercise 7.10 Telephone

In Lisa Iglesias's interview (see Appendix), she describes her collaboration Las Hermanas Iglesias. Read that interview, and then find a drawing partner to work with. Start by each of you making a drawing to exchange with each other. Next, create a drawing inspired the drawing you've just been given. Repeat the exchange three times, and then display these collaborative drawings. See how clearly, or not the works link to each other.

Exercise 7.11 Changing Scale

Sometimes it can be helpful to draw your subject not only in a variety of media, but also in a variety of scales. Try drawing your subject with chalk on a sidewalk and then make the same drawing on a napkin with a pen. Notice how scale and media change the drawing. Has this process helped reveal any essential elements of your drawing?

Exercise 7.12 Engaging a Device

In Justin Lee Martin's interview (see Appendix), he mentions the use of devices that map and record our body's movements. You can see an example of this type of device on the accompanying website (http://RemixingAndDrawing.com). Try building a device that maps your body's movement. Use a drawing generated by the device to inspire a series of drawings.

Exercise 7.13 Mixed Media

In her interview, Alessandra Sulpy reminds us that, "... mixed media can really open you up to experimental mark making" (see Appendix). Try selecting a variety of drawing media to create a drawing. For an even more unexpected result, select a combination of traditional drawing media and less conventional drawing media. For example, one might select charcoal and walking as combined drawing media, or blueberries in cream with graphite (see Roz Crews's interview in the appendix).

Play & Brainstorming

Drawing can be hard work—it can take a lot of concentration and time. However, it's easy to lose interest in your drawing practice if you lose your sense of playfulness. These exercises are meant to help you improvise and brainstorm in a constructive way and will help inject a sense of play into your daily drawing practice. **Improvisation** is creating spontaneously without preparation. It is a good way to find unexpected ideas. **Brainstorming** is the process of coming up with as many ideas as possible without judgement. It is a good way of providing many options to choose from. Brainstorming can be written, sketched, or a combination of the two. After brainstorming and improvising, you can work on composing your drawing from your strongest ideas and components.

Exercise 7.14 Mark-Making

All drawings start with making a mark. Mark-making is inherently fun. It's what we do when we trace shapes in the sand, snow, or the dust on the rear window of a vehicle. Select a drawing implement and make as many different marks with it as possible—confident marks, jagged marks, atmospheric marks, grainy marks, etc. See the earlier sidebar for possible media. Review the interviews with Amy Tavern and Megan Hildebrandt, which both discuss repetition and mark-making (see Appendix). Think about **stippling**, which means drawing with dots; **hatching** and **cross-hatching**, which is drawing with a series of parallel and overlapping lines; **scumbling**, which is drawing with scribbled marks; and marks that are inspired by how the medium feels. Fill an entire page in your sketchbook, or if you're making marks on a larger scale, take photos of the marks and put them in your sketchbook for future reference. Experiment with pressure, direction, speed, emotion, and repetition. Marks do not have to remain neat and tidy. Blurring, smudging, and erasing can all create interesting marks too. This playful mark-making can help give your mind a break and may result in some interesting media discoveries.

Figure 7.2 Hugging Lines.

Exercise 7.15 Hugging Lines

Sometimes when we struggle to come up with new ideas, it can be helpful to focus on the abstract and meditative. One way to do this is to create a page of lines that "hug" each other (Figure 7.2). Start by drawing one line across the page—it can be irregular or precise, but you cannot use rulers or tracing materials. Next, draw a line that follows those contours directly next to your first line. Continue until your page is filled with lines. Inevitably, because we are not machines, the lines will morph and change as you progress across the page, creating an undulating effect. This simple repetitive exercise allows the mind to playfully wander.

Exercise 7.16 Altered Mark-Making Tool

Try altering your mark-making tool. If you're using a pen, attach it to a stick or a string. Try holding your pen with a different part of your body (other than your normal drawing hand). Try moving your paper instead of your pen. What happens when you draw with multiple pens bound together? By adding this type of obstacle to your drawing, you will find that you make a wide variety of interesting marks that you could not have made otherwise.

Exercise 7.17 Music

Select music to draw to. Have a smudge-able drawing medium and a couple different erasers at hand. Allow this drawing to be as messy/smudged as you like. Draw according to your stream of consciousness or stream of feelings as you listen to the music. Do not feel pressured to draw things from reality. Play with abstraction as much as you like. Experiment with different types of music and observe how your drawings change.

Exercise 7.18 Move Your Body

A very simple way to refresh your focus and inspire play is to move your body. If you've been drawing for a while, this simple effort can help get your circulation pumping and deepen your breathing, helping to renew your focus. If you're not sure what kind of physical movement to do, here are a simple set of movements that can be easily be done seated or standing.

Start by standing or sitting tall. Then, extend your arms overhead, reaching for the sky. Next, sweep your arms out to the sides and down as you hinge at your hips into a forward fold, letting your back relax completely. Then, placing your hands on your legs, extend your spine out parallel to the floor for a breath before relaxing into the forward fold again. Finally, reverse your first fold—allow the arms to sweep out and up over head—as you come all the way back up. Repeat this series of movements as many times as you like.

Exercise 7.19 Pattern Study

Sometimes a meditative, repetitive exercise is what we need to find a new sense of play. Try creating a new pattern. Read Erin Harmon's interview in the appendix to get a sense of her use of repeated shapes. Your pattern may be made of simple lines, shapes, and dots, or it can be more complex, including representational imagery. Repeat the pattern over an entire page. As you attempt to draw this repeating pattern, you may find that mistakes can reveal new possibilities you wouldn't have otherwise discovered.

Exercise 7.20 Borrow Someone Else's Process

Read the interviews in the appendix of this book and select a process one of the artists describes. Execute that process yourself. For example, Magnolia Laurie discusses a process using a stack of paper, Roz Crews mentions creating a drawing with a sled in the snow, April Childers touches on tracing imagery, Kharis Kennedy uses photocopying and tape, Elisabeth Condon details the process of copying simplified plant forms from Asian instruction manuals, and so on.

Figure 7.3 Samuel Whatley, *Thumbnails* (2012) graphite on paper, 14" x 11". © Samuel Whatley. Color image available at accompanying website - http://RemixingAndDrawing.com.

Brainstorming for subject matter, compositional choices, content, and more are all important and playful parts of the drawing process. You can incorporate drawing into the brainstorming process by substituting quick, small, rough sketches, also known as **thumbnails**, in place of written ideas (Figure 7.3). Artist Megan O'Connor states in her interview (see Appendix), "When I start a piece, I ALWAYS start with a series of gestural thumbnail sketches to figure out my compositional placement." Thumbnail sketching is another instance where it can be helpful to give yourself a time limit to help hold your focus. Remember that anytime you are brainstorming, it's important to avoid judging your ideas and instead record them all as quickly as possible. You will go back and edit the ideas later. The goal of brainstorming is to gather as many ideas as possible—quantity over quality.

Start small at first and then grow more ambitious: try brainstorming 10 thumbnails in 10 minutes, then try increasing the number of thumbnails and limiting the amount of time. You also might try working with a metronome. With each click of the metronome, sketch another thumbnail. Obviously, you need to set the metronome very slow—something around five to ten beats per minute will work well. If you don't own a metronome, there are a variety of online options. Your drawings will be fast and sloppy, and that's ok.

Exercise 7.21 What If...

Instead of timing your brainstorming, sometimes it can be helpful to spend some time cultivating questions such as "What if—?" For example, what if the goal of my drawing was to get people to fall asleep? What if my drawing existed as a series of lottery tickets? What if I only drew with food products? Share your best "What If" questions with the class and continue to cultivate ideas as you hear from others.

Exercise 7.22 What Would ____ Do?

Another good brainstorming question is "What would ___ do?" Start by selecting some parameters for your drawing. For example, you might create a drawing that involves dotted lines somehow. Then, brainstorm how various artists/designers (contemporary or art historical), fictional people, historical people, or individuals from current events would execute this drawing. Consider what particular expertise the person would bring to the problem and what his or her objectives would be. Again, share your results with the class to gather further ideas.

Exercise 7.23 Break the Rules

This brainstorming exercise is about breaking the rules you tend to follow. Start by making a list of ten unwritten rules you seem to follow when you're drawing. For example, "I only think about drawing with materials I have readily available," or "I think about the end result before I start the drawing," or "I draw what I think will get the most approval online." Then, think about the ten rules in your list, why you tend to follow them, and what it would take to break them. Write down your responses, and use this information to change the rules you follow on your daily drawings as you go forward. Repeat the exercise again after a month of drawing with your new "rules." How have your drawings changed?

Exercise 7.24 By the Bounce of the Ball

Another way to add playfulness to your drawing practice is to physically move your body. Find a small ball, like a tennis or racquet ball, and a surface against which you can bounce it. Set up your sketchbook nearby. Similar to the metronome exercise you will sketch ideas between each time you bounce the ball—as soon as you complete a sketch, you must throw the ball again. By adding this physically playful activity, your mind and body will have to focus acutely on your drawing task.

Critique/Reflection

As you produce new work, remember to take time for critique and reflection. This task is relatively easy to do in a classroom setting where you have many viewers to provide feedback. However, even if you are working outside a classroom environment, it is still important to critique your work, both on your own, and by seeking outside voices. Below, you will find a selection of critique and reflection exercises to help in this ongoing process of growth and development.

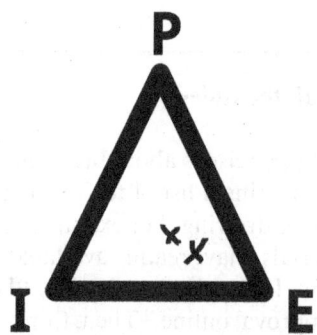

Figure 7.4 Triangle Diagram.

Exercise 7.25 Content-Focused

Communicating content is important in a finished drawing. Sketch a triangle to represent the content of the work. At each apex is a different type of content: physical, emotional, and intellectual (Figure 7.4). Ask yourself and others where the content of this drawing lands, and why. Mark it on the triangle sketch, and notice if your mark/analysis matches that of others. Discuss why your markings may be the same or different.

Exercise 7.26 Audience/Context-Focused

Think about the viewer of the work. What does this artwork assume about its viewer? Think in very basic ways (must they be able to perceive color?) and more complex ways (is an understanding of contemporary art necessary to connect with this work?). What aspects of the work could be changed to appeal to either a wider or narrower audience according to the artist's intentions?

Exercise 7.27 Form-Focused

Start by describing the work you are critiquing without using value-assigning words such as "beautiful," "ugly," "good," or "bad." Simply describe what you see and experience in the presence of the work. For example, observe the colors used, the shapes present, the type of lines or values used, and so on. This is a critique where you can discuss the elements and principles of design and how the work engages the five senses. After thoroughly describing the work, ask what seems to be working well in terms of form, or not, and why.

Exercise 7.28 Subject-Focused

Examine what is being represented in the work, or identify if the work is primarily abstract. Take the time to look at other works addressing the same subject. How does this drawing set itself apart from these other works in terms of subject matter?

Exercise 7.29 Verbal Pairs

Critique in pairs in a classroom setting. Each pair will develop a critique for two works that are not their own, and then report their critique to the class. Upon hearing the critique, artists are welcome to add commentary to further the discussion.

Exercise 7.30 Written Individual

In a classroom setting, use sticky-notes, index cards, or scrap paper to record a one-sentence critique for each drawing, and leave it next to the drawing. Artists are not allowed to repeat any of the critiques already left by the work.

Exercise 7.31 Self-Reflection

Each time you finish a drawing, it is good to reflect on the work. This reflection doesn't have to be done immediately after the work is complete—in fact, waiting a little while may be beneficial in order to gain some perspective. Looking at your own drawing, write down your thoughts based on the following questions:

How does this work use the components of an artwork (subject, form—in terms of the elements and principles of design and the five senses, content, context—in terms of both the artist and the audience)? What works well, and what could be improved?

Exercise 7.32 What Now

A widely used self-reflection exercise is nicknamed, "What? So What? What Now?" This reflection starts with a description of what you have just completed (What?), and follows with the question of why this matters (So What?). The final question is an interesting one: now that you have made this drawing, what is next and why (What Now?).

In this chapter we went through a wide variety of exercises in order to provide opportunities for practice, play, brainstorming, critique, and reflection.

Appendices

Appendix A: Artist Interviews

Becky Alprin | www.beckyalprin.com

1. *Tell us a little bit about your drawing practice.*
   My drawing practice evolved directly from my sculpture and installation practices. My early art training was in two-dimensional disciplines, drawing and painting from life. Somewhere along the line, I began to feel constricted by that pedagogy. I went into an interdisciplinary graduate program with two goals: to experiment with whatever media best served the ideas at hand and to develop a meaty subject matter that could lead me on an extended path of research and art-making. A sculpture and installation practice emerged from this period of study. Some years later, sculpture and installation led me back to a two-dimensional practice, one that is refreshed and invigorated, infused with sculptural ideas. At the start of this drawing practice, I picked up the bits and pieces that made up my sculptures and used them directly in drawings as stencils.
2. *Who/what are some of your influences/sources?*
   Sources of this work include Google Maps and Google Earth, the US Geological Society, and my own photography. The work is deeply influenced by the craft of architectural model making, which I learned at a job I had working as a laser cutting technician during graduate school. There I saw real spaces translated into bit and pieces, put together and pulled apart. I saw the stylized representation of landscape in two dimensions. I saw the same shapes produced and repeated countless times, as ubiquitous as two-by-fours and rectangular windows. It made sense to use my sculptural bits and pieces as stencils, repeated again and again.

3. *How do you see remixing playing a part in your artistic practice?*
   I translate my source imagery into discrete shapes to deconstruct the original, pulling apart buildings and terrain. I pile it up again in my drawings in heaps. The result is landscape drawing made up of countless bits and pieces, and the overriding sense is one of crumbling infrastructure and dystopia. In a sense, I remix information that exists in the public realm about our spaces and environments, questioning the safety and solidity we assume is inherent in them. Our spaces become invisible, like plumbing, until something goes wrong. Right now, Houston and Florida are recovering from a devastating hurricane season. The built environment and its relationship to its surrounding landscape stands out in high relief at this moment.

4. *Do think of yourself as drawing with a particular style(s)? If yes, can you describe it/them?*
   I don't think that I draw in a particular style, but I do feel that the drawings are intentionally highly stylized. There is a near cartoonish quality in the outlining of each shape and in the shapes themselves. This hearkens back to architectural model making, a human-devised sort of game with which we explain spaces to ourselves. Also, the spatial quality of the drawings is highly stylized. It is a shallow space, in which the bits and pieces layer and tile in cascades and piles. The construction of space in traditional Chinese painting and Japanese printmaking has been influential on this work.

5. *Do you have any favorite artists that use remixing?*
   I love the work of Sarah Sze, who also uses hundreds of bits to create her work. Her bits are often industrially produced, readily available, and inexpensive objects used as brushstrokes are used for form, color, and texture, as well as the meaning inherent in the objects themselves. A Styrofoam cup is the right white, the right shape, and also speaks to water, and so can be used in an aqueous landscape and transformed.

Neil Bender | www.pheromonewave.com

1. *Tell us a little bit about your drawing practice.*
   I treat my drawing practice separate from my painting practice, to keep both sides of my brain nimble (ideally…at least that's how I'm treating it). I keep multiple active sketchbooks, usually drawing with Staetdler pigment liners, Sharpie paint markers, and Jelly Roll pens… yet I constantly cannibalize my sketchbooks,

cutting out drawings and affixing them as part of bigger drawings. So all of my sketchbooks have holes cut in them where the drawings were. I get a lot done at school meetings and in bars and on airplanes. I'm also simultaneously cutting pools of flesh and seductive patterns and fabric photos from Purple, Vanity Fair, and W magazines as material to bounce of the drawings, so I always have scraps of color falling out of my cut-up sketchbooks.

2. *Who/what are some of your influences/sources?*
Mike Kelley's all-encompassing oeuvre is an exemplar for me, but particularly his *Hermaphrodite Drawings* and his older black and white drawing installations. Kara Walker's recent ink and graphite drawings and her potent text pieces. Trenton Doyle Hancock's immersive, never-ending drawing work ethic. Matthew Barney's exquisite and elegant (and underrated, IMHO) drawings, in conjunction with his collaged tableaux. Mark Bradford's physical cut-and-paste-and-sanded surfaces. Keith Haring's buoyant joy. Sue Williams's graphic buoyancy and deft touch in reaction to antagonistic sexism and political tumult. Francis Bacon's piles of trashed photographs and monographs as fodder for his visually violent paintings.

3. *How do you see remixing playing a part in your artistic practice?*
I love recontextualizing a drawing or an image, displacing it and having it bump up against a new surface or new image on a new surface. That new relationship is always startling and unexpected, and gives me a visual and visceral jolt. That's the fun in looking at Christian Marclay's album cover images; one move, and one juxtaposition can yield wildly disorientating results. So sampling, remixing, and recombining a multitude of sources—whether explicit or implicit—is an inherent part of my work. We ingest culture and regurgitate in some way that one hopes makes the discourse richer and pleasant (all though we all have different attitudes about pleasure).

4. *Do think of yourself as drawing with a particular style(s)? If yes, can you describe it/them?*
I usually draw with ink, whether with a pen or brush, so there is a slight graphic edge to the work. I identify with the kind of detail and elocution of drawers like Hans Bellmer, Philip Guston, and Heather Benjamin. Hatching and cross-contour lines and long, languid contour lines. It's a kind-of thrift store, hand-me-down version of Pontormo and Leonardo.

5. *Do you have any favorite artists that use remixing?*
Most of the ones in the second question above, but I'd add Robert Rauschenberg's erotically-charged Combines, and Kanye

West. I've been listening to the "Dissect" podcast, which is a great analysis of the ingredients in the soup Kanye makes on "My Beautiful Dark Twisted Fantasy"...everything from subliminal hooks to overt sampling to respeeded percussion to nimble lyrical references both personal and cultural. I come from an era and culture of the mix tape, where one creates and curates a sonic and psychological atmosphere...and I tend to think of music visually too. A Tribe Called Quest, Public Enemy, and Wu Tang Clan all have approaches I admire as much as the aforementioned visual artists.

April Childers | www.aprilchilders.com

1. *Tell us a little bit about your drawing practice.*
   In some works, I print out images from the internet and trace them, in other cases I loosely reinterpret existing images with line for painting later. In a perhaps more "pure" way, I use drawing as a way to physically and conceptually show and describe distance and space. Sometimes, I'll have ideas for pieces that I have to get down quickly on paper. I will draw them quickly, almost as a "note to self." This allows them to begin an existence but, immediately afterwards, I'll see my drawing and get so distracted by the drawing itself that the original idea gets moved to a back burner. Sometimes the "note to self" is a real bubble buster.
2. *Who/what are some of your influences/sources?*
   Cosima von Bonin, Mike Kelley, Raymond Pettibon, Pieter Bruegel the Elder, urban environments/architecture, set design, older cartoons and animations like those produced by the Van Beuren Studios, horror movies, how comedy is produced rather than the comedy itself, TV and movie and their production, Liz Craft, how creativity exists inside of academic and commercial spaces, I'm sure I'm going to think of several others and want to add to this later. The list is always expanding, as it should.
3. *How do you see remixing playing a part in your artistic practice?*
   I keep thinking of remixing as taking existing imagery or environments or even genres of thought and resembling them, kinda like the teleportation scene in *Space Balls* (which has been an ongoing reference for me) where Mel Brooks's character gets "remixed" in a sense. Every time I think of this scene, I remember it wrong. I think of the character's butt being reassembled to the front part of his body, where he can see how large his ass really is. In the

actual film, it's kinda the opposite. It is intended to depict that his ass remains in its original place, however it is his head that is now backwards. Memory and unconscious intentions are important. "Time" travels fast, and we often wanna see the "future" before we can even imagine how to get there. Everything is so very malleable. You can fuck it up and end up looking at your own butt, which is maybe not a bad thing?

4. *Do think of yourself as drawing with a particular style(s)? If yes, can you describe it/them?*
I've always been quietly weary of other artists that seem to draw with such realism and detail. It's so overtly romantic to me. These are the artists that really seem to want to convince me about how deeply they are engaged with the work purely through the act of its highly rendered and finished existence. For whatever reason, I can't trust it. I'm always like "so what?" Also, probably because it's what most people think of as "good" drawing. I don't have the desire to work in such a way. It seems desperate, and I'm too stubborn. If I ever did have that desire, it was a false one, created out of some insecurity. I guess this is one reason why I trace and mimic. I get to address my personal insecurities this way.

I have been trying to change or expand on what drawing is/can be for me. I see created environments, installations, sets, arrangements, and narrative as drawing. Where a thing, element, or part begins and why it ends, like a line. It's kinda like looking at craft and critiquing it in a formal way. The preconceived notion of it is played out through its creation. This is when a "bad" drawing makes good.

5. *Do you have any favorite artists that use remixing?*
Jamian Juliano-Villani, Erica Magrey, Michael Mahachick, Ry Rocklyn, oh man so many. I used to be Davids Altmejd's studio manager, I felt like I was horrible, so I want to say David Altmejd but I won't. Guess I just did.

Elisabeth Condon | www.elisabethcondon.com

1. *Tell us a little bit about your drawing practice.*
On a 2004 trip to Taiwan, I discovered brush pens sold in stationery stores for children to learn characters, which started a serious drawing habit. The brush pens made drawing inviting, more closely related to painting as a "wet" medium. Also, because the marks could not be erased, drawing became experimental, spontaneous.

I drew in Strathmore 5.5 × 8 inch sketchbooks that fit in a large handbag perfectly. I filled the sketchbooks with observations of places while traveling—drawing in parks, from teashops, in shopping malls. I find the immediacy of drawing exhilarating.

Historically in China, copying was valued as a learning method in contrast to the western emphasis on creation and originality. I began to practice simplified plant forms such as bamboo and chrysanthemum from Asian instruction manuals, using ink brushes and rice paper. Stroke order, for example pausing mid-line to pivot the brush or pulling the brush down one side of a form then pushing it up the other, transformed my understanding of the legibility in a gesture. As the simplified plant forms I copied originally derived from calligraphy, their gestures were seen as writing that could be read.

Practicing the plant forms gave me the idea to trace from the sketchbooks along with reproductions of scrolls, wallpaper samples, and fabric patterns on vellum, compressing the travelogues in hand scrolls to single 9 × 11-inch sheets. I also photocopied and collaged my drawings and began to project them in paintings to add hard, artificial line against soft pours of color.

For the last few years I started using landscape format sketchbooks. I've drawn in museums around the world. I drew the Grand Canyon from one side to the other until the shapes locked together like a puzzle. Now I draw flowers and plants. I draw in concentrated bursts. Drawing feels most urgent in a new situation as both a form of digestion and a moving meditation.

2. *Who/what are some of your influences/sources?*
Scroll painting for its holistic symbiosis between gesture and image; textile designs and wallpaper, which translate the natural world into simplified forms that are combined and recombined as a matrix of gestures; the Greeff 1960s design Grosvenor from my mother's sofa; painters Charles Burchfield, Helen Frankenthaler, Huang Gongwang, and Zhao Mengfu come immediately to mind.

3. *How do you see remixing playing a part in your artistic practice?*
Visually, remixing offers speed of delivery in counterpoint to slower methods and tools. The practice accurately reflects our virtual and physical culture. The practice of copying is a form of remixing; tracing certainly is. When I used the (discontinued) Greeff pattern as a reference for a recent group of paintings, I investigated fair use and copyright law. Though in that work the pattern served as a departure point, I asked the designer if he perceived any issues of infringement. Copyright contributes a

conceptual layer on top of the conceptual layer of remixing itself, compressing space into layers even further, creating a virtual dimension in artworks.

4. *Do think of yourself as drawing with a particular style(s)? If yes, can you describe it/them?*
I draw bluntly and illustratively. I would describe my approach as casual but recognizable, probably because of the brush pens. When immersion moves me beyond attachment to image and drawing becomes rhythmic yet precise, I surprise myself.

5. *Do you have any favorite artists that use remixing?*
Mernet Larsen, Zhang Hongtu, Jessica Weiss, Yunfei Ji, and Amy Lincoln are artists I admire who remix in various ways.

Roz Crews | http://rozcrews.info

1. *Tell us a little bit about your drawing practice.*
Before I started kindergarten, I drew a lot of dogs and I could only write fives backwards, so the fives were probably some of my first drawings. Rows and rows of backwards fives, practicing so I could make a forwards five.

After the fives, I drew utopic cat home diagrams, which included floor plans and detailed explanations of how a cat might use each room in the house. I'm allergic to cats, and I think these drawings were a way to connect with my cat loving friends.

By fourth grade, I loved gel pens, so I carried around a purple Crown Royal bag filled with gel pens; at age nine, I didn't know what Crown Royal was, but all my peers had one of these bags, so I asked my parents if they knew how I could get one. I used the gel pens to draw on my friends, and they drew on me, like custom temporary tattoos. We also drew and traded imaginary friends; these drawings were presented as a catalogue and each one came with descriptive texts about the friend's personality traits, height, interests, and other personalized details. As I recall, the creation of imaginary friends helped us explore non-binary identities and notions of friendship with plants or animals outside of social norms in the elementary school.

Gainesville High School was the first place where people tried to teach me how to draw better. Mr. Steinmetz showed how to do two-point perspective, and I convinced him to accept gouache replicas of Renaissance paintings on brown paper bags instead of the perspective assignment. I got a set of Prisma colored pencils and Mrs. Peace, my other art teacher, taught me how to use them. I trusted that she was the right person for this lesson because she once used colored pencils to draw a life-like (but larger than life) portrait of her pet iguana. I was very impressed by her iguana drawing.

In college I started keeping elaborate journals that included contour drawings of almost everything I saw, a record of present moments that instantly became "past." I remember drawing my painting professor, Kim Anderson, mid-sentence, as she explained how to blend colors with oil paint. I also drew a series of every animal I saw during the summer when I worked in a gift shop at Denali National Park. Aside from sketches of people I knew and animals I saw, I made things like a giant charcoal drawing of a collage, which featured two friends and a guy I had a crush on who used to give us free sushi at the restaurant where he worked. I described that drawing as, "A bouquet of Hunter and Hannah coming out of a fist at the dentist."

Alex Velozo was my classmate and favorite artist in college, and I thought the drawings Alex made were the most technically proficient and conceptually compelling I had ever seen; that's when I realized I could never be an illustrator. During this time, I also met Jeffrey Alan Scudder (also known as Jeffrey Heart) who encouraged me to be more free about making art, specifically drawings. He is and was very prolific, drawing constantly and experimenting with different systems for the drawings to emerge. We drew each other using letters of our names and spent nights in Wal-Mart, photographing things and people. In the same year, Milo Moyer-Battick and I created a fake TV show about how to draw. The show was hosted by our personas Jennifer and Bryan who were in love with each other and with drawing. The first drawing Milo and I made together was a public installation at the University of Southern Maine using fans and black garbage bags. I majored in anthropology.

In 2012, I sort of "quit art," not that I ever really started "art" to begin with. I made drawings using sleds in the snow, drawings with blueberries in a bowl of cream, drawings with olives on a pizza. I made one special drawing of two sleeping badgers, a baby on top of a bigger one. It's titled *Seals in Lincoln City*.

In March 2014, I went to New York, and I drew in a sketchbook for the first time in over three years. Maybe it was the pretty spring weather or the unicorn tapestries at the Cloisters, but something shifted during that trip. I drew ghosts shaped like lollipops, kale with tongues, and parrots wearing roller blades, and I decided to go back to school to learn how to make sculptures. When I returned to Oregon where I was living at the time, I met Harrell Fletcher, who asked me why I wanted to make sculptures, and I showed him some drawings I made of baptismal fonts that were meant for birds to go swimming in—bird baths. The tub part of the font was shaped like a Florida swimming pool, painted chlorine blue, and it was the perfect size for a bird. I'm not sure what he thought about that idea, but after our meeting, I joined the MFA program he directs at Portland State University. I became obsessed with non-drawing art practices. But still all my work circles back to communication, and for me drawing is a method of engaging, for cataloguing, for archiving, and for organizing—a language in its own right.

2. *Who/what are some of your influences/sources?*
In 2015 I started working for Kristan Kennedy, the visual art curator at the Portland Institute for Contemporary Art, and the first show I worked on with her was called *No Boundaries*. It was a traveling exhibition of Aboriginal contemporary abstract paintings from Australia, and I sat with the show almost every day that summer. The work by artists Warlimpirrnga Tjapaltjarri, Prince of Wales (Midpul), and Tjumpo Tjapanangka made me think about how far away my home is from my family, paths of power and resistance, secrets, inner selves and outer selves, feminism, and landscapes (both cultural and environmental), and to be honest, before this show, I wasn't sure abstract paintings could make me ponder anything besides colors and shapes.

That experience was influential, and it wasn't just the paintings, but more importantly, the way Kristan attributes meaning to abstraction. She's a painter herself, and she sees and feels the stories and visions and thoughts embedded in marks. She knows whether or not there are feelings in a work of art, and that is a special ability I never knew existed. More than "empathy," but so very empathetic. To be a painter with painterliness, she sees the world in patterns that I don't notice, I'm pretty sure my drawings aren't abstract, but there's a quality that she describes that I'm trying to bring to my work, maybe it's elusiveness or mystery or observation, not sure. Her attention to detail informs how I draw.

I also think there are people like Alice Neel, Elizabeth Peyton, Paul Klee, Cy Twombly, Pablo Picasso, David Shrigley, Margaret Kilgallen, Henry Darger, David Hockney, and Kiki Smith who have empowered me for a long time to draw what is natural to me, and others like Nancy Spero, Kara Walker, Hanne Darboven,

Lawrence Weiner, Johanna Jackson, Chris Johanson, Roman Ondak, Carol Rama, and Leon Golub who I'm hoping will infiltrate my drawing mind more thoroughly.

In one way, I'm hugely influenced by other artists (and writers, too—for example Maggie Nelson, Chris Kraus, and bell hooks who all give my work structure to bounce in), but more immediately, I'm influenced by the people I interact with every day. My everyday (and the people who are part of it) changes frequently—because of moving, because of lifestyle, because of friendship, because of jobs. In the last eight years I've lived in Sarasota, FL, Denali, AK, Washington, DC, Portland, ME, Gainesville, FL, Portland, OR, Santa Fe, NM, and Dartmouth, MA; I've earned two degrees; I've had two-ish serious partners, dozens of friends, several overlapping jobs, thousands of conversations, and over forty projects that have led my life in different directions, designing the drawings for me. Recently I've drawn about being condescended to, ghost sex, my grandma Mildred, a performance I did in New York, fear of non-fears, conversations with Kristan, and infatuation with cars.

3. *How do you see remixing playing a part in your artistic practice?*
Remixing is a confusing word because I think I know what it's supposed to mean, but it reminds me of mixing bowls used in baking—my grandfather was a baker. "Re-mix that! You have to get the flour lumps out." I'm imagining a ton of clear glass mixing bowls on the floor filled with different amounts of ingredients which no one has kept track of and there's too much salt in some, and too much sugar in others, and way too much milk flowing out of seven, and two hundred pounds of flour spilled across the whole area, and that's what remixing is to me. Now to articulate how remixing is part of my artistic practice, I guess we'd have to imagine myself plus 35 other people standing in this bowl room covered in flour and someone is singing. There are 40 drawings of solo cups on the wall, and my 18-year-old self hired someone to explain why having solo cups at parties is an environmental disaster. The disaster-describer is talking slowly through a microphone, wearing a forest green suit made out of polyester which I hate and there's an exceptional 10-year-old writing more and more solo cups on the walls. I would probably call this whole thing a drawing. For me, the problem with identifying a drawing as "remixed" is that it somehow limits and assumes what a drawing is.

I Googled the word to see what other people think remixing is, and I found an article titled "Remix or plagiarism? Artists battle over a Chicago mural of Michelle Obama" written by Derek Hawkins. An urban planner/artist/placemaker Chris Devins stole a digital drawing of Michelle Obama dressed as an Egyptian queen for his public mural. Ethiopian artist Gelila Mesfin originally made the drawing to honor Obama, using a photo by Collier Shorr (who she credits on her website) as the background image, and she posted a video of herself producing the drawing on Instagram, months before the mural was installed. Devins raised $12,000 to produce the mural, originally asking for money to install a black and white graduation photo of Michelle Obama on an exterior wall of a school she attended. After raising the money, he didn't get approval to install the image on the school, so he had Mesfin's drawing (not the image he first proposed), with very minor color changes, painted as a large mural on a building nearby—claiming to the media that the imagery was his idea. When approached by Mesfin and her supporters, Devins called the mural a "'remix' of a piece of art in the way that a DJ remixes songs."

If Devins's plagiarism had a conceptual purpose or twist, maybe I could believe that he "remixed" the young woman's art, but to erase Mesfin's identity and assert himself as the sole author for no other reason except personal gain doesn't seem like remixing as much as a disrespectful form of theft. Mesfin told reporters she thought he should have credited her as the artist of the image from the beginning. I like to believe artists want to be conscious of people's efforts, highlighting original authors and owners, celebrating other people's efforts, noting every contribution, making space for dialogue, trying their best to be honest—I'm thinking of filmmaking, an industry where every single person who helped produced the film is credited, everyone from the director to the boom-mic operator.

I am dismissive of the notion that there are solitary genius artists alone in their studios making masterpieces. In my opinion, everything has been made before, ideas are never new, and people are endlessly influenced by other people; not to mention all the studio assistants who dedicate their lives to making other people's work without acknowledgement by the market, the collectors, the fans, or sometimes even the artists they work for. For me, it makes sense to claim all the efforts and influences as part of the work; at the same time, I recognize that this can be totally complex and maybe impossible, depending on how exhaustive you want to be. The project *Learning to Love You More* by Miranda July and Harrell Fletcher, which asked thousands of people around the world to respond to the same 70 assignments, makes me think about the value of creating something in unison with other people, and that idea makes me wonder, "How unoriginal can I be?" For me, working together feels better than working alone, and I want to consider my influencers as collaborators in a long project about life and everyday experiences, giving those people credit and incorporating their influence or authorship into the work, its title, or its description.

Read Hawkin's full article here: www.washingtonpost.com/news/morning-mix/wp/2017/04/24/remixing-or-plagiarism-in-chicago-a-battle-over-a-mural-of-michelle-obama/?utm_term=.7ff8eb864ad5

4. *Do you think of yourself as drawing with a particular style(s)? If yes, can you describe it/them?*

I think about style a lot, but not usually in terms of drawing. Sometimes I wonder if style is the most effective quality of an artist. Technique is certainly important, and of course, there is craftsmanship! But once we've all figured out technique and craftsmanship, it comes down to style—something a bit harder to learn. To me, style is what the individual or collective brings to the work—the personal touch and the energy. And sometimes style overrides technique or craftsmanship, the style becomes part of the concept or the style accentuates the concept or the style is barring access to the concept. Or in the worst-case scenario, there is style without concept.

Who has the more free-flowing style? The broader strokes (of knowing, of understanding, of thinking, of being). Who has the more rigid style? That's holding me back (from movement, from freedom, from getting it, from being heard, from listening). Who has the more carefree attitude? I mean carefulness and carelessness and patience and playfulness. Who has a more professional style? You look good in a blazer (with gold buttons and matching socks and a watch that no longer tells time and I wish it told futures). There is persistence in knowing what I want. Who is trying too hard? Let go because when you do, you'll fall into the sea where finally you can float (under bridges and through storms), note to self. Try tying your shoes before you get sucked into the escalator.

Adjusting my loose socks, y'all. My eyes are closed. Brushing my bangs. My foot on the chair. My shoes on the table. Raising my hand. Sky light reading. My jeans are too baggy. Cotton instead of rayon. Ankle bruise. Cereal in a glass not a bowl. Walking to the left side of electricity outlet. Seashell night light. Swimming with a kick board. A t-shirt, not a collar. Hello in the morning. Anxiety about the oven. Amateur and clueless, quick and with facts. Laying on the floor while you talk.

5. *Do you have any favorite artists that use remixing?*
I'm pretty sure all my favorite artists are still thinking about the mixing bowls—mixing again to get rid of the lumps when the lumps are a problem, letting lumps be free if they want to. Constantly mixing.

Erin Harmon | www.erinharmon.com

1. *Tell us a little bit about your drawing practice.*
Drawing manifests itself in my practice in a couple ways. I brainstorm compositional shapes in my sketchbook by drawing them over and over. Sometimes it may be a very simple shape like an ellipse, and sometimes it may be much more complicated, but it's always quick and gestural at first. It's not uncommon for me to draw and redraw the same or similar shapes over and over until they feel right or seem used up. I'm seeking something uncanny—often shapes a smidge away from symmetry or balance. These shapes are compositional underpinnings, the bones of what will become a pile. This part feels like brainstorming. Once I understand that outside shape, things get more refined and complex. I introduce other shapes and start to complicate the arrangement of this pile by stacking on top of, inserting into, pouring over, and weaving through the pile with smaller, more complicated components. Sometimes when things get very complicated or the balance I'm looking for is delicate, I may even make templates to get shapes to fit together correctly, and so I make almost architectural drawings for that.

My collage works have drawing inherent in the cut edges of paper components I use. A pen knife or scissors create an edge that is about as definitive as it gets, whether it is planned or intuitive, and this edge has great tension in is. This certainly has spilled over into how I doodle on paper, as I find my hand trying to recreate such an edge even without cutting it. This process also generates two shapes as opposed to one: the positive shape and the negative shape via the cut away fragments. These negative shapes are just as definitive in their edge but much less direct and so exciting. I'm now making work using cut shapes, my shapes but out of slabs of clay. But I also think about these edges and shapes in space which is very related to the kind of gestural drawings I do in my sketchbook.

2. *Who/what are some of your influences/sources?*
   Gardens really interest me, and I like to visit them, but I'm not a gardener. I cultivate houseplants myself, which can have really great shapes and are basically just little piles! I'm a voracious reader and like almost any kind of novel but especially science fiction.

   Lately I have been thinking about Alan Shields, Polly Apfelbaum. Paul Klee, Phillip Taaffe, and Fred Tomaselli are long time influences of my work and still relevant as is the pattern design of Josef Frank. Memphis Milano is a newer (to me) design influence. I love Hockey and as he is, obviously I'm a devotee of Matisse.
3. *How do you see remixing playing a part in your artistic practice?*
   Remixing is an essential part of my process, a key way to investigate what persists to be interesting to me. I think there's always a soup of ideas going on there, and while some may be brand new, the majority are part of a lineage of ideas: attempts to clarify things that I've been curious about for a while and either just haven't gotten to, or have been wrestling with but haven't bested yet. "Why did thing thing work?" "Why was that thing good?" Or when riffing on the work of another artist, "How would that idea or image work in my own language?" Reinterpreting ideas (and forms) is a key exercise for me. Reinterpretation may mean changing fundamental features of an object or image, like material or scale, or it might be really subtle. I remix because it usually leads me to a whole new series of questions, which drive my practice.
4. *Do think of yourself as drawing with a particular style(s)? If yes, can you describe it/them?*
   If you looked in my sketchbook, you'd see two styles: gestural, loopy piles of drawing and also crisp silhouettes. I don't usually draw using color, but deal with that later.
5. *Do you have any favorite artists that use remixing?*
   Kiki Smith is a great mixmaster, reframing images and characters again and again in so many media and at all scales. Guston was brilliant at developing and then pulling from his lexicon of images and surfaces.

Megan Hildebrandt | www.meganlynnhildebrandt.com

1. *Tell us a little bit about your drawing practice.*
   I work primarily in drawing. I am obsessed with line and cannot escape the obsession—even when I paint or do performance-based

works, it always comes back to the line, to the gesture. I love repetition and the way it quiets my anxious brain. I like to use drawing as a way to process time and to try and freeze time. I use animation to slow my process down, focusing on short animations of my daughter or my surroundings. The frame-by-frame slow down is extremely important to my bigger works on paper, which often come quickly.

2. *Who/what are some of your influences/sources?*
My work is quite autobiographical. I often use videos or photographs of my daughter to start off a new work. I also really enjoy letting my "source" dictate the direction of the work—like picking up a different leaf every day for months and letting a drawing slowly build based on the leaves' drying up and color change. I am very influenced by Cy Twombly, Agnes Martin, Frida Khalo, and An Kawara. Right now, I am obsessed with wallpaper and textile design—everything to do with the domestic.

3. *How do you see remixing playing a part in your artistic practice?*
My mom has been having a lot of trouble with her hands—she has developed a tremor and bad arthritis. I wanted to give her my hands, so she would experience relief. I ended up convincing her to let me take photographs of her hands—even though she was extremely self-conscious. I then combined about 50 drawings of her hands, my own hands, and my four-year old daughter's hands in photoshop and ultimately created my own wallpaper the size of a kitchen that is a portrait of all of us. I see each work that is successful as a remix/combination of smaller sketches that I may have worked on for a year or more.

4. *Do think of yourself as drawing with a particular style(s)? If yes, can you describe it/them?*
I think if I have a style, it is that I like to repeat. Repeat: repeat.

5. *Do you have any favorite artists that use remixing?*
I really love Erin Markey and Sarah Kelly—they are more performance though. Also, Wangechi Mutu!

Elisabeth Horan | http://elisabethhoran.com

1. *Tell us a little bit about your drawing practice.*
My collage practice lies somewhere between drawing and sculpture. When I search through magazines for images, sometimes I am searching for something specific, most of the time I am not. I am open to all of the accidental moments.

2. *Who/what are some of your influences/sources?*
   My earliest influences I can remember are Sandy Skoglund and Salvador Dali. Both artists succeed in creating environments into which the viewer can escape.
3. *How do you see remixing playing a part in your artistic practice?*
   I am working on a current series of figures collaged from Yoga Journal and various porno mags. The "Goddesses," as I am calling them while in progress, are a remix of the reigning heteronormative fetishization and commodification of the female body. I am taking the power back by remixing them into multi-limbed figures, which echo deities in Hindu mythology.

   I think every artist uses remixing to a degree. Even every person has this experience in daily life. As William S. Burroughs put it, "our perception is a consumption of cut-ups."
4. *Do think of yourself as drawing with a particular style(s)? If yes, can you describe it/them?*
   My style is surreal, grotesque, funny, and sweet.
5. *Do you have any favorite artists that use remixing?*
   Martha Rosler, Barbara Kruger, Wangechi Mutu.

Lisa Iglesias | www.lashermanasiglesias.com/lisa-iglesias

1. *Tell us a little bit about your drawing practice.*
   I think of drawing as an expansive sensibility that makes visible an interaction between the mind and the body. In my studio, depending on the project, this relationship may amount to tracings of thought, to-do lists, mapping, collage, playing with language, byproducts of material interaction, re-creations of found images, recordings of patterns, translations of thought to image, and other processes. For me, drawing is this very democratic process…it's elemental, amorphous, forgiving, and resistant to categorization. I can work individually or collectively, make videos or works on paper—and throughout think of my practice as rooted in drawing.
2. *Who/what are some of your influences/sources?*
   Found imagery has occupied a large territory in my studio practice—family photos, rodeo and hunting photographs, and diagrammatic illustrations of geology have long been present in each studio (or bedroom, kitchen floor, or office) where I work. Vija Celmins and Tacita Dean influenced me very early on, particularly in regards to thinking about time, re-creation, and the simultaneous sublimation and insertion of the self. Louise Bourgeois has been an inspiration as well, through her writings and

meditations on family, especially now that I'm a mother. Word play and literature also figure in strongly as a source—grammatical structures, narrative devices, and language regularly influence my decision making while drawing.

3. *How do you see remixing playing a part in your artistic practice?*
Remixing plays a part in my practice through a variety of contexts. Collage has consistently appealed to me as an opportunity to harness the charge of found images. Space opens up for conversations between mechanical reproduction and the subjective hand; between original intention and altered associations; and for me, between geological and human time.

In another way, over the past six years, I've begun a combinative approach for installation in which I create a series of drawings—discreet elements that serve as ingredients ready to be remixed and altered each time I install them. Remixing allows me to continuously create new meanings through shifting these elements in their locational contexts and material associations each time I install the work.

My sister Janelle Iglesias and I think about remixing and translation when we work on projects as Las Hermanas Iglesias and Lisa & Janelle Iglesias. We approach remixing as an opportunity to translate ideas into new forms. We do this by passing images and marks back and forth between us or by collectively ushering a sequence of objects or shapes through a series of visual or conceptual filters until an evolution or re-creation develops.

4. *Do think of yourself as drawing with a particular style(s)? If yes, can you describe it/them?*
The style I use to approach an idea depends on the nature of the project. In the past, I focused on attempting to objectively recreate a photo-based image with graphite on paper. This strategy had a lot to do with futility, the relationship between photography and drawing and fulfilling gestures of memorialization. More recently, I've been interested in conflating disparate languages within one space and loosening my control of the media, and so in many ways, an acknowledgment of the haptic nature of the materials and more gestural qualities of the mark have entered the work. In this way, thinking of the paper as a three-dimensional material that can be cut through and as a surface that can accept a multiplicity of approaches has manifested in the studio.

5. *Do you have any favorite artists that use remixing?*
There are so many artists who approach remixing and drawing in exciting ways, so it's hard to identify favorites, and I know I'll be

leaving out many artists whom I admire. Just to mention a handful, I am always inspired by the ways with which Andrea Bowers, Ana Mendieta, Njideka Akunyili Crosby, Joan Linder, Firelei Baez, and Mark Bradford remix materials and ideas.

Kharis Kennedy | http://khariskennedy.com

1. *Tell us a little bit about your drawing practice.*
   Any distinction between painting and drawing for me has more to do with how I handle a particular medium vs. the poor, innocent medium itself. When creating an under-painting, although using a brush and paint, I rely on gestural line-drawing techniques; in other words, I draw with paint. But then again, even in an under-painting situation, I will inevitably interrupt a line with the more painterly approach of blocking in and pulling out form.

   I don't ascribe to many absolutes, so it bears noting that I consider the small pieces that I paint with sumi ink to be drawings. For me a drawing is about an immediacy and finality of a mark. It is absolutely intimidating: ink says whether you've got it or you don't.

2. *Who/what are some of your influences/sources?*
   For the past three years, *W* and *Vogue* (don't buy the English language versions—the French is so much better. And not just because you can't understand it. The whole layout is better.) Magazines have provided my core of polished source images. When a fashion rag starts to betray me, I jump ship, but these two have been holding steady. They both feature a good number of spreads where items that stylists either own or have created are incorporated and drive the shoot's mood. I like building off of the creativity and energy of stylists as fellow artists.

   As an artist living in the Caribbean, I meld these polished images with raw imagery. I am particularly drawn to Carnival images of individuals who use costuming and other modes of outer adornment to register political resistance. I relate to using fashion, i.e. one's outer adornment, to register resistance.

3. *How do you see remixing playing a part in your artistic practice?*
   At heart-level my paintings, performances, and filmed imagery is built off "composites." I create my composites by assembling source images onto the plain brown cardboard insides of cereal boxes. (Correct: I consume a notable amount of cereal.) Most often I make black and white working photocopies of the source images and save the originals. This allows me the freedom to forget

what designer colors existed in reality and select color based on my emotional intent. To adhere the photocopies to the cereal boxes, I use either clear packing tape, black duct tape, or silver duct tape. In all my work I like an immediacy and brutality. I treat the composites with respect; they are pieces within themselves. I often use the taping itself as a painterly, blocking gesture. The composite itself is a piece.

4. *Do think of yourself as drawing with a particular style(s)? If yes, can you describe it/them?*
   The composites drive the mood of my paintings and performances. Although the composites are almost always black and white, the overall tone does not create a contemplative, noir effect because my assemblages typically portray emotions at an edge: one person at the brink of utilizing vulgarity as a strategy, another caught in the moment right before they enter into violent action, and so on. My composites are all ultimately psychological self-portraits of myself at precipice moments: I am too well cared for, too well-heeled, and yet too easily discarded.

5. *Do you have any favorite artists that use remixing?*
   I always drew inspiration from Leon Golub's immediacy of gesture. But then when I heard he had a filing system for source images?!?!? Let's not pretend.

Magnolia Laurie | www.magnolialaurie.com

1. *Tell us a little bit about your drawing practice.*
   My drawing practice is a space of unguarded exploration. I consider it an essential part of my studio practice, though I only occasionally exhibit my drawings. I draw in series, in that I prep a stack of paper or materials and let myself move through ideas in a pretty intuitive way. I never try an idea one time, but rather work around the idea several different ways—that's the importance of drawing for me. For me, drawing is immediate, playful, full of salvaged and accepted accidents that build into ideas. Sometimes these ideas are directly used in my paintings, sometimes I continue to explore them in the drawings until I understand how and why they seem important or relevant.

2. *Who/what are some of your influences/sources?*
   History, current events, poetry, climate change, social dynamics, art history, contemporary art, the internet—I don't tend to have one source that I repeatedly use, but am constantly gathering images, stories, and bits of information to combine and reconfigure.

The idea of context and how it alters and impacts meaning is something I am very interested in.

3. *How do you see remixing playing a part in your artistic practice?*
My physical and digital collages are probably the most literal representation of "remixing" but I would say it actually happens throughout my work in that I am always gathering information from different sources and trying to see how they can fit together to create something new. I am often trying for a duality and ambiguity that allows the work to read as both political and personal, serious and witty, intentional and playful.

4. *Do think of yourself as drawing with a particular style(s)? If yes, can you describe it/them?*
I don't think I do.

5. *Do you have any favorite artists that use remixing?*
There's so many, but to name just a few:

Las Hermanas Iglesias, René Treviño, Andrea Chung, Njideka Akunyili Crosby, Pamela Phatsimo Sunstrum, Molly Springfield, Kara Walker, Ellen Gallagher, Fred Owens, Jessica Stockholder, Kerry James Marshall, Neo Rauch, Luc Tuymans, Mamma Andersson

Justin Lee Martin | www.justinleemartin.com

1. *Tell us a little bit about your drawing practice.*
My work starts with a drawing. I gravitate towards drawing for immediacy, love for pictorial space, and process. My drawings range from graphite on paper to devices that map and record our body's movement. Often, found materials make their way into my drawings, and this adds additional layers of meaning. Like painting, I think of drawing in terms of construction, deconstruction, and rebuilding in any order. This can be understood as an analogy of the ever-changing landscape whether it be physical or social.

2. *Who/what are some of your influences/sources?*
Maryann Bonjorni has had the most influential impact on me as an artist. It was in Maryanne's studio classes at the University of Montana that the world as I knew it became more profound. She opened my perception to pictorial space and fostered my interest and connection of growing up in the "Wild West." As a young artist, I remember the first time I saw Sigmar Polke's monumental painting *Mrs. Autumn and Her Two Daughters*, 1991, at the Walker Art Center. I was taken back. The complex spaces, narrative, and emotional investment were all there. I also find Brian

Goeltzenleuchter's work fascinating in that it blurs boundaries between sight, smell, social, and physical.

3. *How do you see remixing playing a part in your artistic practice?*
I frequently visit secondhand stores looking for materials to include in my work. Most of the time it's a found drawing or painting that eventually ends up altered in my painting/drawings. My interest in low-art stems from the art I saw in my youth on the walls of homes such as wildlife, cowboys, and picturesque landscapes that romanticized the "West," in particular, themes of Montana. These works were so falsely inaccurate to the life I have experienced that they fascinated me.

4. *Do think of yourself as drawing with a particular style(s)? If yes, can you describe it/them?*
Not really. It's always changing.

5. *Do you have any favorite artists that use remixing?*
Maryann Bonjorni, Brian Goeltzenleuchter, Francis Alÿs, Buster Simpson, Richard Tuttle, Marcelo Moscheta, Cameron Robbins, Johanna Calle.

Guen Montgomery | http://guenmontgomery.com

1. *Tell us a little bit about your drawing practice.*
My drawing practice is two-fold. On one hand I draw as a first step, often as a means to another end. Often this means sketching to prepare imagery for prints and drafting plans that help me to visualize complex projects. These drawings, especially those that end up as prints, often involve a lot of erasing, reworking, and multiple iterations before I am satisfied with the finished drawing.

I also draw for myself. Unlike my print work, this kind of drawing tends to be free-associative, intuitive, and unedited. These images, which exist somewhere between doodling and journaling, are graphic hyper-simple line drawings of elongated cat-like animals, usually done with a pen. I try to draw this way to give my mind and eye a break from the sequential, process-based way I usually work. These drawings allow me to tap back into the playful satisfaction of childlike doodling and reenergize me when I start to feel confined by other projects. I don't allow myself to edit or erase these drawings and allow them to come into being imperfectly without judging the quality of one over another.

2. *Who/what are some of your influences/sources?*
My studio work is broadly influenced by human characters around me. Frequently my work investigates the ways we build our

identities around the accumulated stories we tell ourselves about who we are. This means that I look at identity in terms of gender, sexuality, family mythology, regional culture, and personal histories. My drawings that become prints pull from a wide range of sources, many familial and photographic. My line drawings are much more stream-of-consciousness, although I see similarities to Keith Haring's vibrating figures and Ray Johnson's bunnies.

3. *How do you see remixing playing a part in your artistic practice?*
Although I don't use collage or direct appropriation much in my work, I do think everything I do stems from a mental remix of all the visual input I'm exposed to. Like most artists I subconsciously borrow from the things I've seen, sometimes without realizing that I am picking up things here and there. I also remix my own work—one idea will sprout an offshoot that feels new but borrows conceptually or visually from past works.

4. *Do think of yourself as drawing with a particular style(s)? If yes, can you describe it/them?*
My drawings that result in finalized prints strive for some degree of realism and are not heavily stylized. However, even when I aim to avoid strong stylization, some personal drawing conventions are always present. For example, I love line work and tend to think linearly instead of in masses and volumes. I like fine linear details, subtle changes in line weight, intricate textures, and patterns, so I emphasize these over the illusion of the dimensional space, even when aiming to depict reality. My more playful, graphic, linear creature drawings are much more stylized. This stylization results from the freedom I give myself to depart from representational depiction. They are loose, elongated, and strange because I allow myself to be loose when drawing them. I love playing with slightly abstracted linear forms and try not to edit myself, often filling entire pages with these experiments.

5. *Do you have any favorite artists that use remixing?*
In terms of successful remixing, I recently saw the Meow Wolf *House of Eternal Returns*, an interactive, immersive art installation in Santa Fe, New Mexico. The themes in this massively collaborative art installation, which fills a 20,000 square foot defunct bowling alley, are familiar. Thematically Meow Wolf borrows from popular culture fantasy tropes including creepy Queen Anne style domestic spaces, haunted forests, mythically large beasts, and an X-files inspired storyline that asks the viewer to take part in unlocking the mystery at the heart of the work. Nonetheless, the entirety of the experience feels strikingly new.

I think this freshness is due to the combined vision of the 135 artists behind the piece and their masterful collaborative remixing. It stands out to me as an impressive contemporary example of cultural collage.

Meghan O'Connor | www.CurLyMeg88.com

1. *Tell us a little bit about your drawing practice.*

    I've always loved animals, and since childhood, I have drawn them. These animals (usually song birds, as of late) are rooted in the narrative and observational drawing. When I start a piece, I ALWAYS start with a series of gestural thumbnail sketches to figure out my compositional placement. Because my drawings are so detail oriented, I like to work through my ideas as quickly and crudely as possible before I invest in an image. I also prefer to work with life-size elements, so I draw a lot of small items, such as song birds!

    I love drawing birds, not only because it affords me the time to focus on their details, but also because they easily adapt to technological changes around them. They are fragile with hollow bones and they have personality traits with which I can find connections to people around me and my life experiences. When I choose my subject, it is not only for their visual characteristics, but also in relation to the bird's personality or social traits, and how these traits connect to the theme that I am currently addressing. In addition to this, I just LOVE drawing birds and their feathers. There's so much to be offered in their actual and implied textures; so, it is a self-indulgent behavior at times!

    When I talk about my drawing practice, I should mention that it is not upon paper. I draw on Bavarian limestone with grease crayons to create lithographs (a type of fine print). This surface gives me the option to work both additively and reductively in very physical ways. I can apply materials to the stone and then scratch details with an etching needle that has a drawing tip much smaller than the tip of a sharpened graphite pencil. I love it! Once the drawing is complete, it is coated in gum Arabic and processed chemically for printing. To ink the image, the surface of the stone is dampened with a sponge and rolled up with an oil-based ink. The water in the sponge is attracted to the non-image areas and rejects the oil-based ink of the roller, and the ink is attracted to the greasy drawing. After it is properly inked, paper is laid down on the stone and the pressure of the printing press transfers the ink from the surface of the stone onto the paper.

2. *Who/what are some of your influences/sources?*
   Historically speaking Francisco Goya and Heironymous Bosch are two major influences. My high school art teacher had this calendar hanging in her office with an image of Bosch's *Garden of Earthly Delights*, and I was smitten. When I was in graduate school, I visited Museo del Prado and got to see this piece in real life, and I was first struck at how small it was; and then I immediately found myself crying. I cried again later that day, when I saw that Goya's works-on-paper wing was closed for cleaning! Ultimately, I respect both of these artists: Goya, for making works that address the harsh realities of his time as opposed to turning a blind eye, and Bosch, for his love of detail, imagination, and for representing the darker side of human nature.

   I love a lot of contemporary printmaking as well, but Kathryn and Andy Polk come to mind first and foremost. They create lithographic drawings which are narrative. The imagery is not only visually rewarding and technically rendered, but also deals with stereotypes, personal experiences, and is very socially and culturally engaged. On top of this, they are amazing teachers, for which I have a lot of respect.

3. *How do you see remixing playing a part in your artistic practice?*
   Remixing definitely plays a part with the amount and types of source imagery that I incorporate into my work. For every piece, I combine multiple images to create one composition. For example, in *Love it's Bones*, I started with an image in my head of a rotund house-wife-bird cleaning the house, holding babies, trying to balance her domestic and life duties with her own wants and needs. I then gathered images of an obese man's belly, images of domestication such as aprons and a Roomba, and geriatric imagery such as walkers and canes, and of course, birds! I take all these references that have certain meanings on their own, and combine them in a Frankenstein-like manner to create a new context or idea.

   Currently, with my newest project, I am approaching remixing a different way. In summer 2017, while at the artist residency, Arquetopia, in Puebla, Mexico, I started gathering my source imagery in a more community—interactive manner. While at the residency, I worked in a community print shop at the Museo Erasto Cortes; and, while there, I walked around with a container of words on paper. The words I have written so far are: "hierarchy, attack, resist, guilt," and "I'm sorry," inspired by my research into The Museum of Religious Art (The Former Convent of Santa Monica) in Puebla. While at the printmaking museum, I would ask people to take a word, read it, and interpret it with a hand gesture that I could photograph. Now, I am grouping and remixing these images to show MY interpretation of each of these words, by drawing them as lithographs, and laser engraving sculptural elements into wood. As I move forward with this new body of work, I will continue to gather gestures from the community, building upon these previous experiences.

4. *Do think of yourself as drawing with a particular style(s)? If yes, can you describe it/them?*
Yes: neurotic! Ha! All joking aside, I love creating detailed illustrative imagery, usually animal-based, but not always. My work is detailed in the sense that I aim to record everything I observe about forms and their textures. This is a very controlled way of working and can drive one crazy after some time; so, I like to balance drawing these implied textures with the use of actual textures, creating blind embossments with collagraph and found materials, such as feathers, hair, and wires, because sometimes it's just fun to cut, glue, and get your hands dirty!

5. *Do you have any favorite artists that use remixing?*
I love any work involving exquisite corpses, Surrealism, and Dada, especially the collage work of Hannah Höch and Max Ernst, because of the mix of animals and humans, as well as their keen awareness of scale. These artists create a new context for interpretation through these unexpected combinations!

Anytime we can work in a way that promotes conversations and collaboration, I think it will benefit us as artists and our ability to work together as a team, which is essential for the survival of humankind. When I have my students do group/collaborative projects, I like to say that it's like going to a potluck: you get there, and there's all this food on the table. Every person brings something, and that's our ideas that we can share. You can try a little bit of everything and decide what you like. Who knows, you might be surprised about that broccoli casserole, or maybe you don't like it; but, you understand its value and now you know it's there. Either way, chance comes into play, and there are possibilities for new insights, new connections, and new remixes, if you wish.

Julia Oldham | www.juliaoldham.com

1. *Tell us a little bit about your drawing practice.*
I work primarily in video and animation. My animated work typically combines live action video with hand drawn elements that

can allow for a fantastical character to be inserted into a real environment. For example, I have made video in which I, as a performative character, encounter wild animals, enter a dream world, or visit outer space. The process of drawing for my animated work is very repetitive and labor intensive, and through the act of slowly building animation frames and developing animated characters through their actions, I will often come up with new stories and narrative twists for my videos. In that sense, drawing becomes a means of working through a problem and brainstorming for solutions. More recently, drawing itself has become a more visible part of my practice, and I've been showing drawings alongside videos in exhibitions. I have a show coming up this fall that will be entirely drawing. The finished drawings I make serve a similar function to drawing in my animations in that I can create impossible narratives. Right now, I'm working on a series of self-portraits as a werewolf.

2. *Who/what are some of your influences/sources?*

   As a student, I wanted to be a scientific illustrator, so some of my artistic background is in illustration. I'm incredibly drawn to illustration and to artists who use the language of illustration in their work, such as contemporary artists Marcel Dzama and Amy Ross. I am in love with Rockwell Kent's 1930 illustrations of Moby Dick and Russian illustrator Yuri Vasnetsov's illustrations for children's books, which he made around the same time as Kent's pieces. I also read a lot of graphic novels. One of my very favorites is Julia Gfrorer's Black is the Color, about a man adrift at sea and his hallucinations of mermaids as he lay dying. Her drawing style is scratchy and strange, and it creates such a beautiful sense of doom.

3. *How do you see remixing playing a part in your artistic practice?*

   I primarily use remixing as a way of creating alternate realities. I blend video with animation and photography with drawing to mix the real and the unreal together. In my video Laika's Lullaby, about a Soviet space dog who was the first living creature to enter orbit, I combine hand drawn animation of Laika with public domain footage and photos of outer space and spacecraft to tell a story that could never be shot as a live action work. I like the combination of imperfect animation that really shows my hand with photography, because the two very different visual languages create a totally separate space that isn't entirely real or unreal. I'm interested in the work of drawing itself being part of the content of these animated works. Right now, I'm working on a series of Werewolf Selfies in which I combine my own instagram selfies with bits and pieces of photos of wolves I find on the internet and I use digital drawing as a means of seamlessly connecting the imagery to make myself into a werewolf. This combo of photo collaging and drawing makes for some pretty weird portraits. Sometimes the lighting is off on different elements of the collage, creating a dreamlike quality, and sometimes the level of detail differs between the selfie and the wolf body part. But when I connect the pieces by painstakingly drawing fur and skin, I create a believable but bizarre creature that seems to inhabit the real world. I get to remix myself this way too—shapeshifting into something other.

4. *Do think of yourself as drawing with a particular style(s)? If yes, can you describe it/them?*
I have borrowed techniques from numerous historical book illustrators and usually think of my drawings as being storybookish. They are very representational, usually of women interacting with animals, and tightly drawn in black and white like you might expect in a Victorian storybook. My digital drawings are a more realistic representation, in which I used photoshop to fool the viewer into believing something that's not real. I'm not sure what one calls this style—is there such thing as "Photoshopped" style?

5. *Do you have any favorite artists that use remixing?*
I recently discovered Swedish artist Simon Stalenhag, who creates super photorealistic digital paintings of bizarre futuristic creatures and structures in banal landscapes. His images are often of rural American neighborhoods and natural landscapes that are reminiscent of Dorthea Lange or Robert Adams, but incorporating a giant alien spaceship or a huge robot into the scene so that it looks perfectly natural. This is the aesthetic I'm feeling really excited about right now—collisions of unlikely aesthetics such as sci-fi and the pastoral!

Charles Sommer | www.charlessommerart.com

1. *Tell us a little bit about your drawing practice.*
I almost always begin an idea with a graphite drawing or group of drawings. For me drawing is the most direct and efficient way to communicate and clarify whatever blurry image happens to pop into my head. I rarely use direct external source imagery, so for me drawing is the best way to shorten the distance between a thought or memory and the page. The drawings are usually

textures, forms, and artifacts derived from landscape. Often, I will cut up and reassemble the drawings into larger collage studies. The studies then get transformed into paintings, animations, or sculptures. However, the process can circle back around. I might redraw forms that appear in the animations as a result of the digital transformation process and then use those drawings in more collages to create additional landscapes. It is this potentially endless cycle of self-referential drawing, transformation, and redrawing that interests me. Working this way keeps the world, and work, within its own universe and provides endless sources for creating new forms all while revolving around drawing.

2. *Who/what are some of your influences/sources?*
Science fiction, pseudo sciences, 'real' and theoretical sciences, landscapes, technology, and digital spaces.

3. *How do you see remixing playing a part in your artistic practice?*
I guess I see the process of transforming my initial drawings into more complex images as a form of remixing. I also think that collage is definitely a form of remixing. When I make a collage, the hardest part of the process is to know when to stop cutting drawings up and when to stop gluing them together. In addition to the physical remixing of drawings in my process, there is always a remixing of any idea, influence, and frankly anything I consume or am thinking about. Although I really think that is what every artist does. Artists will consume just about anything, they will remix those ideas, and put it back out into the world disguised as art.

4. *Do think of yourself as drawing with a particular style(s)? If yes, can you describe it/them?*
I'm not really sure, although my drawing is pretty tight and controlled—I guess you could say that's my style.

5. *Do you have any favorite artists that use remixing?*
Katherine Ryals, Ian Chang, Brian Belott, Mitch Patrick are a few that come to mind.

Molly Springfield | http://mollyspringfield.com

1. *Tell us a little bit about your drawing practice.*
My work consists primarily of graphite drawings that use printed texts as their source material.

   My projects usually start with library-based research. During the research phase, I gather books and other documents that I photocopy. Through the process of photocopying and re-photocopying, I enlarge texts and images. I use the final photocopy as a source material for my drawing. My imperfect hand, together with the added visual noise and texture created during the photocopying process, adds an additional layer of meaning and information.

I often use drawing to consider drawing's relationship to other media, especially photography and writing. I'm interested in the history of information and representation and the way that key moments fundamentally transform the way we see and experience the world.

2. *Who/what are some of your influences/sources?*

As a young artist, I was very much influenced by the work of nineteenth-century American trompe l'oeil painters, like John Peto. By tricking the eye into thinking that a painted object is real, trompe l'oeil paintings challenge a viewer's visual security. When it's very convincing, you doubt your ability to discern what is real and what isn't. It forces you to take an active role in looking. The work is self-referential. In trompe l'oeil, you often see representations of flat objects—like an envelope or a sheet of paper—on a flat service. This calls attention to the painting as a flat surface, it's not trying to be a window into a three-dimensional space like a landscape or a history painting.

Trompe l'oeil artists were making representational work that is about the idea of representation. In the era of photography, when painting becomes less about illusion, it's a very deliberate decision to try to trick a viewer when illusion is no longer the primary goal of the medium. I think you can make the argument that trompe l'oeil was one of the first conceptual art forms.

During graduate school I studied the Conceptual art practices of the 1960s and 1970s in depth for the first time. That work had a profound influence on my work and development as an artist—particularly language-based work by artists like Mel Bochner, Lawrence Weiner, Lee Lozano, and Susan Hiller.

It radically shifted my frame of reference, from the history of painting and drawing, to the history of conceptual art. It forced me to really think about the relationship between text and image and to focus more on process and concept rather than only seeing my work in terms of a specific disciplinary tradition. I was especially interested in the way Conceptual artists used language—more in the way that writers do. The visual qualities of text weren't completely abandoned, but they weren't the primary focus.

But, like a lot of contemporary artists, I don't just look to the history of art for inspiration. In particular, I look to literature and the history of information science for inspiration and sources.

My past projects have drawn on the writing of Marcel Proust and W.G. Sebald, for example, and the life and work of the early twentieth-century Belgian information scientist Paul Otlet.

3. *How do you see remixing playing a part in your artistic practice?*

I take existing texts, and through the photocopying process, I change the meaning of those texts through repetition or reordering of words or phrases. An additional layer of content is added by reproducing the image by hand. This happens on several levels—a literal one because I make mistakes and those mistakes introduce new visual information—and on a conceptual level, because I'm creating an original, permanent object from something that is meant to be disposable.

Part of the intent of my work is to get at the problematic nature of reproduction and originality, but also to question the usefulness of what I'm doing. It seems like a pretty futile process, so what's the value of the labor I'm putting into it?

Increasingly, my work blurs the line between the visual and written. I've come to think of my most recent drawings as pieces of writing that are experienced visually. The source material for these drawings come from my ongoing project The Marginalia Archive—which I started in 2007 and collects contemporary examples of marginalia into a functioning archive that viewers can access and contribute to. The archive can function as a stand-alone work, but I use the contributions as source material for drawings that are exhibited alongside the archive or on their own.

My most recent archive-derived drawings follow the rise and fall of a reader's handwritten underline as it moves from panel to panel beneath a sentence. The resulting drawings form—or "remix"—new words and phrases between panels, functioning on one level as found, abstract poetry. But the emphasis on the underline confuses the relationships between writing and drawing, facilitating the viewer's ability to switch between experiencing the drawing as a visual artwork and as a written document.

4. *Do think of yourself as drawing with a particular style(s)? If yes, can you describe it/them?*

I would describe my drawing style as observational. Others might describe it as photorealistic, and I would be comfortable with that description. Photographs—or photocopies—are part of our observable world the same as any other object that you could look at and draw. Artists make observational drawings at least in part to make sense of the world around them and give their viewers insight into how they see the world.

5. *Do you have any favorite artists that use remixing?*
   I'm a big fan of early Dadaist collages, particularly Kurt Schwitters and Hannah Höch. But, considering your broader definition of remixing and looking to contemporary art, I think Fred Wilson's *Mining the Museum*, which takes objects in existing museum collections and redisplays them in ways that expose the inherent biases of our cultural institutions, is an excellent example. Also, pretty much anything by Cornelia Parker. Her project *Brötean Abstracts* is a particular favorite.
   Women artists who work with text and "remix" to varying degrees that I've been inspired by include Susan Hiller, Fiona Banner, Jen Bervin, Erica Baum, and Deb Sokolow.

Ian Stewart | http://bigmention.com

1. *Tell us a little bit about your drawing practice.*
   As a designer I've more or less relied on drawing out ideas to get things moving in the right direction since before I can even remember. But rather than sitting down and telling myself "it's time to draw now," I feel that this process is fully integrated into my life in a manner that I'm not even conscious of it. Drawing is not necessarily a practice for me but simply something I do every single day akin to any other daily activity we aren't hyper aware of.
2. *Who/what are some of your influences/sources?*
   I'm inspired by everything I see. Whether they're beautiful and creative or ugly and boring. Of course seeing art at galleries or in museums is very inspiring, but I find just as much inspiration in everyday life. Graffiti tags, store fronts, abandoned buildings, well done designs, poorly done designs, the internet, random people I come into contact with, old books and magazines (and new ones too). I could go on, but I think the point is given. As far as specific influences go I'm very inspired by Robert Rauschenberg's entire body of work, the pop artists, and a lot of random vintage textbook and manual designers.
3. *How do you see remixing playing a part in your artistic practice?*
   I suppose my entire practice is based upon remixing. With my visual art being essentially collage it wouldn't be possible without source material to work from. However in a not so literal sense, I also remix thematically as well, taking an idea and reforming it to fit my needs.
4. *Do think of yourself as drawing with a particular style(s)? If yes, can you describe it/them?*

I think I'd probably note myself as being of the simplistic style of drawing, maybe cartoon or comic book style as those were my biggest influences growing up.
5. *Do you have any favorite artists that use remixing?*
One could argue that any artist is "remixing" if not literally then in essence, but I feel like the ones who are more openly regarded as such that I tend to hold in high regard would be: Andy Warhol, Robert Rauschenberg, KAWS, Banksy, Sanghyuk Moon, Shepard Fairey, Barry McGee, Keith Haring, and Ai Weiwei.

Alessandra Sulpy | *www.alessandrasulpy.com*

1. *Tell us a little bit about your drawing practice.*
My drawing practice almost always mixes with my painting practice, and almost never materialize as a "drawing" in the purest sense of the word. My work incorporates mixed media, utilizing paint, collage, assemblage, and drawing materials like pastel, graphite, or marker. I love the concept of "drawing" with paint and "painting" with traditional drawing materials—and that mixed media can really open you up to experimental mark-making. A fat, painted mark shouldn't have to exist independently from a thin, drawn line, and there's real beauty in that; have a love affair with your materials, and don't worry about categorising your finished work.
2. *Who/what are some of your influences/sources?*
I am a big fan of pop art, especially figurative artists like Larry Rivers and Peter Blake. They are masters of synthesizing bold, abstract moments with representational, objective ideas. Even though all representational art has elements of abstraction, when that balance is more evenly split between what is seen and what is imagined, there's a new and exhilarating vibrancy. We can take that to the level of material—something unexpected and fresh is born by playing with what we use. Take Peter Blake's assemblage paintings, which are in a category of their own—they are all at once figurative, abstract, painting, drawing, sculpture, and collage.
3. *How do you see remixing playing a part in your artistic practice?*
Admittedly, I have a little of the magpie mentality of always looking for the next new and exciting thing to add to my paintings; I've used lenticular prints, glowing neon wire and flashing lights, laser cut pieces, and shaped canvas. I love fusing something new with something traditional like oil paint, and as my paintings often

depict a bygone era, the idea of new vs old is always alluring. I also try not to be too precious with my art—sometimes you have to sacrifice your favorite parts or "kill your darlings" for something to work. I recently finished an oil painting on paper, and when it was done, I realized it had more potential cut up and re-formatted into a sculptural piece. I lost some parts of the painting I liked and had worked hard on, but it became a more successful piece in the end.

4. *Do think of yourself as drawing with a particular style(s)? If yes, can you describe it/them?*
I like it colorful, loud, and energetic! I like to throw down a mark and leave it there until the end—and I like to spend hours working up one small area. Layering is important to me, and when I use both oil and water-based media, I have to think about how to build up those layers without the piece falling apart in 15 years. I am rarely too nitpicky, even when working realistically. My studio is a pretty horrific mess when I'm in the middle working, as I'm surrounded by the many mediums, tools, paints, markers, etc. that I need at a moment's notice.

I love the beautiful strangeness of Italian Mannerism, the looming commotion of Precisionism, and the vibrant immediacy of Pop. As an artist, I am guided and informed by my influences and am the sum of what I observe and adore.

5. *Do you have any favorite artists that use remixing?*
Jerome Witkin uses unexpected color, and his work looks at once like pastel drawings and oil paintings, which feels fresh and vibrant. Larry Rivers is a master of mixing abstraction with figurative representation, and Tom Wesselman does all sorts of groundbreaking work, including drawings in steel. I love contemporary artists Jenny Morgan and Karim Hamid for their fresh and colorful takes on figurative work. I admire these artists because of their ability to shuffle genres and show us something new and original.

Amy Tavern | www.amytavern.com

1. *Tell us a little bit about your drawing practice.*
Drawing, or my use of line, is an integral part of my artistic practice. I use line to create tangible, or physical, connections between what I see and feel, and I draw to recollect and recreate my memories. Drawing happens with pen or pencil on paper or through the act of folding, creasing, or incising. I also use sewing and thread

to create lines. Sometimes my hands directly engage with my materials, while other instances I use a tool like an X-Acto knife or bone folder. The process can be additive or reductive, and I often use chance and performative actions to activate it. I tend to use labor-intensive, solitary methods and work minimally, relying on order and repetition to guide me. I allow the lines in whatever form or material to layer and accumulate on their own.

2. *Who/what are some of your influences/sources?*
My immediate surroundings wherever I am, Iceland and California in particular, walking and what I observe while walking, geological phenomena (specifically plate tectonics and earthquakes), seismograms and EKGs, maps and cartography, implied lines such as the line of the horizon, the work of Norman McLaren, Richard Long, Michelle Stuart, Anni Albers, and Mono-ha.

3. *How do you see remixing playing a part in your artistic practice?*
I use the same crooked line over and over in my work, whether drawn with a pen on tracing paper or wrinkled and folded over the surface of Tyvek. I move this line from piece to piece as if it's leading me somewhere, as if I am searching for something. I have no idea what it is I'm looking for or where the line is taking me, and, most likely, it will never end at a specific place or time. Remixing allows me to examine and reexamine and, ultimately, to see things in a new way.

4. *Do think of yourself as drawing with a particular style(s)? If yes, can you describe it/them?*
My style is abstract, minimal, gestural, and repetitive.

5. *Do you have any favorite artists that use remixing?*
Kara Walker, Park McArthur, Tacita Dean, and Jumana Manna...

Appendix B: Suggested Breakdowns of Exercises/Assignments/Readings

15 Weeks

Week 1: Read this book, analyze the style of drawings using the cheat sheet, start answering Paul Thek questions, do privilege exercise(s), refresher drawing exercises in class

Week 2: Start some of the suggested daily drawing exercises, do more self-analysis to further build your collection of sources and influences, select artists you'd like to use for copy/synthesize/morph—everyone can do an in-class verbal report on a single selected artist to help others widen their collection of influences

Week 3: Everyone presents their artists and starts first master copy, critiques first master copy, and selects artist for next master copy (for weeks 3 and on, feel free to sprinkle in your favorite exercises from the text as you like—some will feel more or less relevant in each drawing program)

Week 4: Everyone starts their second master copy, critiques second master copy, and does brainstorming for how they might synthesize their two different master copies; consider additional readings (see continued reading list)

Week 5: Everyone starts synthesis drawing, critiques synthesis drawing, does brainstorming for how they will morph the drawing into their own creation; consider additional readings (see continued reading list)

Week 6: Everyone starts morph drawing, critique morph drawing, selects artists they'd like to use for second round of copy/synthesize/morph—again, everyone can do an in-class verbal report

Week 7: Everyone presents their artists and starts first master copy, critiques first master copy, and selects artist for second master copy; check to ensure everyone is still building a good collection of sources and influences (this should be ongoing)

Week 8: Everyone starts second master copy, critiques second master copy, and does brainstorming for how they might synthesize their two different master copies; consider additional readings (see continued reading list)

Week 9: Everyone starts synthesis drawing, critiques synthesis drawing, does brainstorming for how they will morph the drawing into their own creation; consider additional readings (see continued reading list)

Week 10: Everyone starts morph drawing, critiques morph drawing, selects artists they'd like to use for third (final) round of copy/synthesize/morph—again, everyone can do an in-class verbal report

Week 11: Everyone presents their artists and starts first master copy, critiques first master copy, and selects artist for next master copy; consider additional readings (see continued reading list)

Week 12: Everyone starts second master copy, critiques second master copy, and does brainstorming for how they might synthesize their two different master copies; consider additional readings (see continued reading list)

Week 13: Everyone starts synthesis drawing, critiques synthesis drawing, does brainstorming for how they will morph the drawing into their own creation

Week 14: Everyone starts morph drawing, critiques morph drawing. Everyone begins preparing for their artist talks, which will include presentations of sources and influences and description of their style.
Week 15: Artist Talks

10 Weeks

Week 1: Read this book, analyze the style of drawings using the cheat sheet, start answering Paul Thek questions, do privilege exercise(s), refresher drawing exercises in class

Week 2: Start some of the suggested daily drawing exercises, do more self-analysis to further build collection of sources and influences, students select artists they'd like to use for copy/synthesize/morph—everyone can do an in-class verbal report on a single selected artist to help others widen their collection of influences

Week 3: Everyone presents their artists and starts first master copy, critiques first master copy, and selects artist for next master copy (for weeks 3 and on, feel free to sprinkle in your favorite exercises from the text as you like—some will feel more or less relevant in each drawing program)

Week 4: Everyone starts their second master copy, critiques second master copy, and does brainstorming for how they might synthesize their two different master copies; consider additional readings (see continued reading list)

Week 5: Everyone starts synthesis drawing, critiques synthesis drawing, does brainstorming for how they will morph the drawing into their own creation; consider additional readings (see continued reading list)

Week 6: Everyone starts morph drawing, critiques morph drawing, selects artists they'd like to use for second round of copy/synthesize/morph—again, everyone can do an in-class verbal report

Week 7: Everyone presents their artists for the second round and starts first master copy, critiques first master copy, and selects artist for second master copy; check to ensure everyone is still building a good collection of sources and influences (this should be ongoing).

Week 8: Everyone starts second master copy, critiques second master copy, and does brainstorming for how they might synthesize their two different master copies; consider additional readings (see continued reading list)

Week 9: Everyone completes synthesis and morph drawings, critiques, preps for artist talks
Week 10: Artist Talks

Appendix C: Continued Reading / Viewing List

American Library Association's Fair Use Evaluator. Accessed December 21, 2017. http://librarycopyright.net/resources/fairuse/

Australia Council for the Arts. Protocols for Working with Indigenous Artists. Accessed August 6, 2017. www.australiacouncil.gov.au/about/protocols-for-working-with-indigenous-artists/

Band, Jonathan and Jonathan Gerafi. *The Fair Use/Fair Dealing Handbook* [international equivalent of Fair Use]; Accessed December 21, 2017. http://infojustice.org/wp-content/uploads/2015/03/fair-use-handbook-march-2015.pdf

Center for Media & Social Impact; Accessed December 21, 2017. http://cmsimpact.org

College Art Association's "Code of Best Practices in Fair Use for the Visual Arts"

Copy This Podcast by Kirby Ferguson via the Re:Create Coalition. Accessed December 21, 2017. https://soundcloud.com/user-864134809

Creative Commons. Accessed December 21, 2017. https://creativecommons.org/licenses/

Evans, David, Ed. *Appropriation*. MIT Press, 2009.

Eyers, Pegi. What Is Cultural Appropriation? Stone Circle Press. Accessed August 7, 2017. www.stonecirclepress.com/blog-9658-ancient-spirit-rising/what-is-cultural-appropriation

Ferguson, Kirby. "Resources." *Everything Is a Remix Site*. Accessed October 8, 2016. http://everythingisaremix.info/references/

Four Factors of Fair Use (actual legal language). Accessed December 21, 2017. www.copyright.gov/title17/92chap1.html#107

Foster, John. "Under the Influence: Drugs, God and Politics in Self-Taught Art." *Art21 Blog*. Accessed October 3, 2016. http://blog.art21.org/2010/11/29/under-the-influence-drugs-god-and-politics-in-self-taught-art/

Gagnon, Rachel. "New Flash Points: Influence." *Art21 Blog*. Accessed October 3, 2016. http://blog.art21.org/2010/11/01/new-flash-points-influence/

Hareen, Natilee. "Knight's Heritage: Karle Haendel and the Legacy of Appropriation, Episode One, 2000." *Art Journal OPEN*. Accessed October 8, 2016. http://artjournal.collegeart.org/?p=6929

Hareen, Natilee. "Knight's Heritage: Karle Haendel and the Legacy of Appropriation, Episode Two, 2012." *Art Journal OPEN*. Accessed October 8, 2016. http://artjournal.collegeart.org/?p=7115

Hareen, Natilee. "Knight's Heritage: Karle Haendel and the Legacy of Appropriation, Episode Three, 2013." *Art Journal OPEN*. Accessed October 8, 2016. http://artjournal.collegeart.org/?p=7235

Intellectual Property Issues in Cultural Heritage Project, 2015. *Think Before You Appropriate. Things to Know and Questions to Ask in Order to Avoid Misappropriating Indigenous Cultural Heritage.* Simon Fraser University: Vancouver. Accessed December 21, 2017, http://www.sfu.ca/ipinch/sites/default/files/resources/teaching_resources/think_before_you_appropriate_jan_2016.pdf

Johnson, Maisha Z. What's Wrong with Cultural Appropriation? These 9 Answers Reveal Its Harm. *EverydayFeminism*. Accessed August 7, 2017. http://everydayfeminism.com/2015/06/cultural-appropriation-wrong/

Kleon, Austin. *Steal Like an Artist: 10 Things Nobody Told You about Being Creative.* Workman Publishing Company, 2012.

McLeod, Kembrew and Rudolf Kuenzli. *Cutting across Media: Appropriation Art, Interventionist Collage, and Copyright Law.* Duke University Press, 2011.

Moloney, Meredith. "Neuenschwander and Influence." *Art21 Blog*. Accessed October 3, 2016. http://blog.art21.org/2010/11/24/neuenschwander-and-influence/

Uwujaren, Jarune. The Difference between Cultural Exchange and Cultural Appropriation. *EverydayFeminism*. Accessed August 7, 2017. http://everydayfeminism.com/2013/09/cultural-exchange-and-cultural-appropriation/

Wolfson, Elizabeth. "Music and Art." *Art21 Blog*. Accessed October 3, 2016. http://blog.art21.org/2010/12/07/music-and-art/

Appendix D: Books and Websites for Finding Drawing Artists to Copy

Women Who Draw. Accessed December 21, 2017. www.womenwhodraw.com/

The Drawing Center. Accessed December 21, 2017. www.drawingcenter.org/

Fukt Magazine. Back-issues available online. Accessed December 21, 2017. http://fukt.de/contributors/

The Sketchbook Project. Accessed December 21, 2017. http://blog.sketchbookproject.com/

Aristides, Juliette. *Classical Drawing Atelier.* Watson-Guptill, 2006.
Beverly Hale, Robert. *Drawing Lessons from the Great Masters.* Watson-Guptill, 1989.
Buck, Stephanie. *Master Drawings from the Courtauld Gallery.* Paul Holberton Publishing, 2012.
Butler, Cornelia and Catherine Zegher. *On Line: Drawing through the Twentieth Century.* The Museum of Modern Art, 2010.
Cauteren, Philippe Van and Martin Germann. *Drawing. The Bottom Line.* Mercatorfonds, 2016.
Dexter, Emma. *Vitamin D: New Perspectives in Drawing.* Phaidon Press, 2005.
Garrels, Gary. *Drawing from the Modern, 1945–1975 (HC).* The Museum of Modern Art, 2005.
Germann, Martin and Elsy Lahner. *Drawing Now.* Hirmer Publishers, 2015.
Hauptman, Jodi. *Drawing from the Modern.* The Museum of Modern Art, 2004.
Hopman, Laura. *Drawing Now: Eight Propositions.* The Museum of Modern Art, New York, 2002.
Ibarra, Anna and Marc Valli. *Walk the Line: The Art of Drawing.* Laurence King Publishing, 2013.
Kovats, Tania. *Drawing Book: A Survey of Drawing: The Primary Means of Expression.* Black Dog Publishing, 2007.
Maltreat, Roger. *Drawing People: The Human Figure in Contemporary Art.* D.A.P./Distributed Art Publishers, Inc., 2015.
Phaidon, Editors of. *Vitamin D2: New Perspectives in Drawing.* Phaidon Press, 2013.
Rattemeyer, Christian. *Compass in Hand: Selections from the Judith Rothschild Foundation (HC).* The Museum of Modern Art, 2009.
Sell, Stacey and Hugo Chapman. *Drawing in Silver and Gold: Leonardo to Jasper Johns.* Princeton University Press, 2015.
Stout, Katharine. *Contemporary Drawing: From the 1960s to Now.* Tate, 2015.
Trustees of the National Gallery. *The Draftsman's Art Master Drawings from the National Gallery of Scotland.* National Gallery of Scotland, 2000.
Wold-Simon, Linda and Carmen C. Bambach. *An Italian Journey: Drawings from the Tobey Collection, Correggio to Tiepolo.* Metropolitan Museum of Art, 2010.
Yamaguchi, Yumi. *Warriors of Art: A Guide to Contemporary Japanese Artists.* Kodansha USA, 2007.

Appendix E: Selected Drawing Artists for Master Copies

Franz Ackermann
Lady Aiko
Marijn Akkermans
Derek Albeck
Laylah Ali
Jowhara Alsaud
Kai Althoff
D-L Alvarez
Francis Alÿs
Gemma Anderson
Ryoko Aoki
Kevin Appel
Ida Applebroog
Patrick Arrasmith
Martin Assig
Kate Atkin
Frank Auerbach
Charles Avery
Silvia Bächli
Jeanette Barners
Matthew Barney
Adam Batchelor
Sabina Baumann
Jeffrey Beebe
Dale Berning Sawa
Joe Biel
Robert Blechman
Peter Blegvad
Matt Bollinger
Shannon Bool
George Boorujy
Mary Borgman
Michael Borremans
Louise Bourgeois
Carine Brancowitz
Marc Brandenburg
Jesse Bransford
Cecily Brown
Fernando Bryce
Tim Burton
Richard Busk
Ernesto Caivano
Brooke Cameron
Los Carpinteros
Virginia Chihota
Marcos Chin
Sevda Chkoutova
Michael Cho
Sandra Cinto
Francesco Clemente
Fernanda Cohen
John Copeland
Russell Crotty
R. Crumb
Amy Cutler
Susan D'Amato
Leonardo da Vinci
Adam Dant
Henry Darger
Tacita Dean
Edgar Degas
Katharina Denzinger
Louise Despont
Mark Dion
Bailey Doogan
Penelope Dullaghan
Avram Dumitrescu
Roisin Dunne
Sam Durant
Albrecht Durer
Marcel Dzama
Memed Erdener
Simon Evans
Inci Eviner
Shepard Fairey
Faith47
Simon Faithfull
Diane Fitch
Eduardo Flores (Bayo)
Jacques Floret
Tim Foley
Richard Forster
Erin Fostel
Anthony Freda
Phil Frost
Franziska Furter
Marcel Gahler
Ellen Gallagher
Steven Gammell
Alberto Giacometti
Dryden Goodwin
Rachel Goodyear
Antony Gormley
Jason Greenberg
Anna Sigmond Gudmundsdottir
Cai Guo-Quiang
Philip Guston
Trevor Guthrie
Daniel Guzman
Sebastian Hammwohner
Trenton Doyle Hancock
Martin Hanford
Hayuk
Travis Head
Mercedes Helnwein
Eva Hess
Warren Holder
Christian Holstad
Paul Hoppe
Roni Horn
Lauren Alyssa Howard
Sterling Hundley
Cho Duck Hyun
Seb Jarnot
James Jean
Yun-Fei Ji
Qiu Jie
David Jien
Li Jin
Reece Jones
Kerstin Kartscher
Tomoko Kashiki
Kashink
Sagaki Keita
Mike Kelley
William Kentridge
Toba Khedoori
Margaret Kilgallen
Don Kilpatrick III
Daehyun Kim
Sol Kjok
Jenny Kostecki-Shaw
Juul Kraijer
Dan Krall
Jesse Kuhn
Dr. Lakra
Ricardo Lanzarini
Juliette Le Roux

Appendices 113

Matthias Lechner
Jinju Lee
Martha W. Lewis
Ulrike Lienbacher
Laurie Lipton
Graham Little
Susan Loeb
Mark Lombardi
Mindaugas Lukosaitis
Emilio Valdes
Miss Van
Chris Van Allsburg
Rinus Van de Velde
Marcel van Eeden

Vincent Van Gogh
Heather van Wolf
Rinus Vande Velde
Sandra Vásquez de la Horra
João Vilhena
Banks Violette
Jorinde Voigt
Wolfe Von Lenkiewicz
Moritz von Schwind
Amelie Von Wulffen
Kara Walker
Stephen Walton
Andy Ward

Kyle T. Webster
Ellen Weinstein
Olav Westphalen
Andrea Wicklund
Martin Wilner
Martin Wilner
Richard Wright
Frank Lloyd Wright
Katharina Wulff
Sun Xun
Eric Yahnker
Taizo Yamamoto
Daniel Zeller
Hong Chun Zhung

Glossary

Appropriate to incorporate the work of others—either in full or in part—into a new creative work
Artist talk a formal presentation describing the artist, their art, and how and why they make their work by providing context and insight for the audience
Assemblages three-dimensionally built collage
Brainstorming the process of coming up with as many ideas as possible without judgment
Capitalist Realism a movement inspired by the imagery in newspapers and magazines and influenced by Pop Art in America
Collage the act of combining a variety of materials, not just fine art supplies, to create compositions
Content the meaning or impact of the work
Context the set of factors surrounding the creation and display of the work, and it can include a wide range of elements, such as age, class, race, gender identity, sexual identity, geographic location, religion, culture, political affiliation, and so on
Copyright legal protection of creative objects
Creative Commons license allows various types of reuse under certain parameters
Cross-hatching and hatching drawing with a series of parallel and overlapping lines
Cubism An art movement that purposefully ignores the traditions of perspective and naturalistic representation through a variety of tactics, including showing multiple views of a subject simultaneously
Cultural appropriation the process of an individual from a powerful and dominant culture adopting elements from a culture systematically oppressed by the dominant culture; sometimes also known as cultural misappropriation

Glossary

Cultural misappropriation the process of an individual from a powerful and dominant culture adopting elements from a culture systematically oppressed by the dominant culture; sometimes also known as cultural appropriation

Culture Jamming a tactic used to subvert or critique political and advertising messages and promote progressive change, closely related to situationism and détournement.

Cut-up methods cutting the words and rearranging them by chance, rendering them nonsensical

Dada An art movement focused on anti-war and anti-materialistic middle-class ideas

Détournement the appropriation of prevalent words and images from dominant culture and turning them against the system

Digital Millennium Copyright Act (DMCA) stated that internet service providers were vulnerable to prosecution if they didn't take down content that copyright owners complained about, regardless of whether the work falls under the category of fair use

Fair use the legal use of materials under copyright for certain socially valuable uses

Fan art art specifically created for a community of fans of an existing body of work, oftentimes related to movies, shows, cartoons, lines of toys, and so on

Forgery the crime of replicating another artwork as closely as possible and attempting to pass it off as the original

Form the sensorial experience of the work (how does it look, sound, smell, taste, and feel); includes the media as well as the arrangement of the compositional elements

Gift economy a system of exchange based on the concept of conveying goodwill or establishing a bond between people without expectation of any immediate or future reward

Hatching and cross-hatching drawing with a series of parallel and overlapping lines

Improvisation creating spontaneously without preparation

Influences other artists, designers, and/ or visual culture producers who stand out as impactful to the artist

Intellectual property the idea that our culture is a market, and everything of value should or can be owned by someone

Loss-aversion when creators feel it is ok to copy others, but not ok for others to copy what they created

Master copy the act of replicating a master work as closely as possible

Morph transform

Musique concrete a way of constructing music by mixing recorded sounds

Nonrepresentational a work that does not depict a specific identifiable person, place or thing

Parody an imitation of the style of a particular writer, artist, or genre with deliberate exaggeration for comic or critical effect

Photomontage a composite photograph made of various other photographs that have been cut and pasted to create a new composition

Pop Art An art movement focused on bringing images from pop culture and mass media into artworks in order to challenge mass consumption of everyday culture

Privilege an unearned benefit or advantage we carry with us throughout life due to some aspect(s) of our identity, such as race, gender, age, sexual orientation, religion, class, etc.

Public domain the collection of works *not* protected by copyright that can be used and built upon by other thinkers and creators

Punk Movement A musical and cultural movement that borrowed détournement and other subversive political pranks

Readymade a manufactured non-art object that is altered, perhaps only slightly, to reframe it as an artwork

Remixing combining various works together to create something new

Research the process of locating information in order to reach new conclusions

Sampling including clips from other musical works in a new musical work, which are repeated and/or rearranged

Satire the use of humor, irony, exaggeration, or ridicule to expose and criticize people's stupidity or vices, particularly in the context of contemporary politics and other topical issues

Satirist a person who uses humor, irony, exaggeration, or ridicule to expose and criticize people's stupidity or vices, particularly in the context of contemporary politics and other topical issues

Score directions for an action

Scumbling drawing with scribbled marks

ShareAlike a requirement of some Creative Commons licenses, mandating further sharing under the same agreement as the work spreads

Situationism An art movement founded by Guy Debord and focused on critiquing capitalism

Sources pieces of culture not directly related to art or design, such as—but not limited to—nature, dreams, or current events

Stippling drawing with dots

Style the distinctive visual quality or physical characteristics of an artwork
Subject what the artist is portraying such as people, places, and things
Synthesis combination
Thumbnails quick, small, rough sketches
Zines self-published, small-circulation magazines or books that often contain original and/or appropriated text and images reproduced via photocopier

Index

24 hour psycho 12

A Tribe Called Quest 76
Adbusters 12
Ai Weiwei 104
Albers, Anni 106
Alice in Wonderland 17, 18
Alprin, Becky 31, 73
Altmejd, David 77
Alÿs, Francis 93
Anderson, Kim 80
Android 16
animals 41, 79, 80, 93, 95, 97–99
animation 15, 50, 60, 76, 87, 97, 98, 100
AP *see* Associated Press
Apfelbaum, Polly 86
Apple 11, 15, 16
appropriation 7–16, 23, 28, 34, 48, 94
architectural 31, 73, 74, 76, 85
archive-derived *see* archives
archives 1, 20, 30, 102
archiving (practice) 1, 3, 81
Art Assignment, The 33
Art Deco 2
Art:21 33
artist talk 3, 57, 58, 108, 109
Artist to Artist 33
assemblage 9, 10, 12, 91, 104
Associated Press 13, 24
audio 9, 11, 33

Bacon, Francis 75
Baez, Firelei 90
balance 85, 96, 97, 104
Baldwin, James 12
ball 70
Banksy 41, 104
Banner, Fiona 103
Barbie Liberation Organization 12
Barney, Matthew 75
Baum, Erica 103
Beat 10
bell hooks 82
Bellmer, Hans 75
Belott, Brian 100
Bender, Neil 31, 74
Benjamin, Heather 75
Berlin Radio Fair 9
Bervin, Jen 103
best practices *see* Code of Best Practices in Fair Use for the Visual Arts
Beyoncé 30
Bichlbaum, Andy 12
Big Cartel 62
Billboard Liberation Front 12
Blake, Peter 104
Blakley, Johanna 24
blend 80, 98
Bochner, Mel 101
body 30, 64, 66, 67, 70, 76, 88, 92
bold 2, 104
Bonanno, Mike 12
Bonjorni, Maryann 92, 93
bookstore 32
Bosch, Heironymous 96
Bourgeois, Louise 88
Bowers, Andrea 90
Bowie, David 30

Bradford, Mark 75, 90
Braque, Georges 8
Brauntuch, Troy 11
breathing 67
Brooks, Mel 76
brush pens 77, 79
brushed 2
Burchfield, Charles 78
Burroughs, William S. 10, 88
Byzantine 42

Calle, Johanna 93
Capitalist Realism 10
Carlson, Chester 10
cartography 106
cartoon 27, 74, 76, 104
Celmins, Vija 88
chalk 63
Chang, Ian 100
Chaplin, Charlie *17, 18*
charcoal 39, 50, 64, 80
Charlie Brown Christmas special 17
Chic 11
Childers, April 1, 68, 76
Chronicle Book 60
Chung, Andrea 92
Cinderella 17
class (academic) 13, 25, 33, 36, 50, 58, 60, 69, 72, 106, 108
Code of Best Practices in Fair Use for the Visual Arts 22, 23
collage 8–11, 13, 75, 78, 80, 85, 87–89, 92, 94, 95, 97, 99, 100, 103, 104
College Art Association 22, 23
colonialist 7
color 35, 40, 41, 46, 60, 62, 71, 74, 75, 78, 80, 81, 83, 86, 87, 91, 98, 105
colored pencils 79, 80
comic 32, 104
complex 2, 62, 67, 71, 83, 85, 92, 93, 100
composition 1, 5, 8, 9, 14, 32, 39, 46–50, 68, 85, 95, 96
Condon, Elisabeth 6, 68, 77
conflict 30
consumption 10, 30, 31, 88
content 1, 12, 14, 15, 27, 39–42, 44, 47, 48, 68, 71, 72, 98, 102
context 1, 3, 8, 13, 14, 31, 39–42, 44, 47, 48, 71, 72, 89, 92, 96, 97

contrast 1, 5, 6, 28, 44, 46, 78
Cooper Union 33
Cooper, Merian C. *17*
copy/synthesize/morph 3, 46, 49, 50, 59, 106–108
copyright 3, 6, 11–16, 19, 20, 22–28, 78
copyright act 20–22
Cornell, Joseph 9
Cosima von Bonin 76
cost 22, 33
Craft, Liz 76
crayon 95
Creative Commons Licenses 19, 25, 26, 28, 109
Creative Commons *see* Creative Commons Licenses
Crews, Roz 1, 47, 64, 68, 79
Crimp, Douglas 11
critique 1, 3, 8, 10–12, 23, 39, 50, 58, 59, 70–72, 77, 107–109
Critique Cheat Sheet 43
Crosby, Njideka Akunyili 90, 92
cross-hatching 65
culture 2, 6–16, 19, 23, 24, 30, 32, 41, 42, 75, 76, 78, 94
culture jamming 11, 12
current events 2, 30, 31, 69, 91
cut-up 9, 10, 75, 88

Dada 9, 10, 97, 103
daily 31, 59–62, 64, 70, 88, 103, 106, 108
Dali, Salvador 25, 88
Darboven, Hanne 81
Darger, Henry 10, 81
Das schöne Mädchen 9
DaVinci, Leonardo 75
Dawe, Gabriel 50
Dean, Tacita 88, 106
Debord, Guy 10
détournement 10–12
digital drawings 83, 99
Digital Millennium Copyright Act 12
direction 65, 87, 103
Disney 15, *17, 18*
DMCA *see* Digital Millennium Copyright Act
documentary 3, 15, 20, 28, 33
Dore, Gustave *17*

dreams 2, 30, 31, 98, 99
Duchamp, Marcel 9, 25
Dzama, Marcel 98

edge 75, 85, 91
elements and principles of design 39, 50, 71, 72
emotion 1, 30, 41, 48, 65, 71, 91, 92
Endless Summer, The 25
Engineering 9
environment 70, 74, 76, 77, 81, 82, 88, 98
erasers 66
erasing 65, 77, 83, 93
Erma Series: Leaving 38, 39
Ernst, Max 97
Etsy 62
etude aux chemins de fer 9
everything is a remix 28
exquisite corpse 62, 63, 97

failure 30
faint 2
fair use 3, 6, 8, 12, 13, 19, 20, 22–26, 28, 46, 78
Fairey, Shepard 13, 24, 41, 104
fan art 27
Fantasia 17
fantasy 94
Faust 17
fictional 69
figurative 104, 105
flag 41
Fletcher, Harrell 81, 83
Flintstones, The 17
fluid 31
focus 66–68, 70, 87, 89, 95, 101
food 30, 31, 69, 97
form 1, 11, 14, 16, 39–42, 44, 46–48, 71, 72, 74, 78, 90, 102, 106
Fountain 9
Fox, Justine 7, 55
Frank, Josef 86
Frankenthaler, Helen 78
Fritz the Cat 17

G.I. Joe 12
Gagosian gallery 13
Gallagher, Ellen 92
gallery 3, 13, 32, 41, 103

Gallon, Dale 34
Gap, The 25
Gaylord v. United States 23
gel pen 79
gender *see* privilege: gender identity
geographic location 14, 42
geography 30
Germany 9, 10
gesture, gestural 48, 68, 78, 85–87, 89–91, 95, 97, 106
Gfrorer, Julia 98
Ghost in the Shell 25
gift economy 26–28
Girl Scouts 16
globalization 7
God Save the Queen 11
Goeltzenleuchter, Brian 93
Goldstein, Jack 11
Golub, Leon 82, 91
Gongwang, Huang 78
Good Times 11
Google 16, 73
Gordon, Douglas 12
Goya, Francisco 96
GPS drawings 39
graffiti 30, 31, 41, 103
graphic novels 98
graphite 39, 40, 50, 64, 75, 89, 92, 95, 99, 100, 104
Guo-Qiang, Cai 50
Guston, Philip 75
Guthrie, Woody 9

Hamid, Karim 105
Hamilton, Richard 10
Hancock, Trenton Doyle 75
Hansen, Hadley 52, 53
Happy Birthday 16
Haring, Keith 75, 94, 104
Harmon, Erin 85
Hart, Brian 50
hatching 65, 75
Heart, Jeffrey *see* Scudder, Jefferey Alan
Hildebrandt, Megan 65, 86
Hiller, Susan 101, 103
hip hop 11, 12
history 6, 7, 30, 91, 101
Höch, Hannah 9, 97, 103
Hockney, David 81

Index

Homage to the Romantic Ballet 9
Honeymooners, The 17
Hongtu, Zhang 79
Hope poster *see* Fairey, Shepard
Horan, Elisabeth 87
horror 76

Iglesias, Lisa 63, 88, 89, 92
illustration 28, 88, 98
Impressionism 2
index cards 72
indigenous 7
Insertions into Ideological Circuits 11
inspiration 2, 30, 31, 36, 88, 91, 101, 103
Instagram 13, 83
intellectual 1, 41, 71
intellectual property 16
interpersonal 30
iPhone 16

Jackson, Johanna 82
Jazz 9
Jefferson, Thomas 14
Ji, Yunfei 79
Jobs, Steve 15
Johanson, Chris 82
Johnson, Ray 94
Joyce, Don 11
Juliano-Villani, Jamian 77
July, Miranda 83
Just What Is It That Makes Today's Homes So Different, So Appealing? 10
Jüttner, Franz *17, 18*
juxtaposition 6, 11, 75

Kawara, An 87
KAWS 104
Keaton, Buster *17*
Kelley, Mike 12, 75, 76
Kelly, Sarah 87
Kennedy, Kharis 68, 90
Kennedy, Kristan 81
Kent, Rockwell 98
Khalo, Frida 87
Kilgallen, Margaret 2, 3, 81
King Kong 17
Klee, Paul 81, 86

Kraus, Chris 82
Kruger, Barbara 11, 88

Lady Gaga 30
landscape 40, 50, 73, 74, 78, 81, 93, 99–101
Lange, Dorothea 99
Larsen, Mernet 79
Las Hermanas Iglesias 63, 89, 92
Laurie, Magnolia 67, 91
law 6, 12, 15, 19, 26, 78
LeFave, Kallie 27, 51
Lessons from fashion's free culture 24
Letham, Jonathan 2, 16, 30
Levine, Sherrie 11
Ligon, Glenn 12
Lincoln, Amy 79
Linder, Joan 90
line 46, 65–67, 69, 71, 75–78, 86, 87, 90, 93, 94, 104–106
linear 2, 94
literature 30, 89, 101
location 2, 14, 32, 33, 42, 61, 62, 89
Long, Richard 50, 106
Longo, Robert 11
loose 2, 76, 94
loss-aversion 16
Lozano, Lee 101

magazine 10–12, 75, 87, 90, 103
magnetic tape 9
Magnetophone K1 9
Magrey, Erica 77
Mahachick, Michael 77
Mahoney, Heather 4, 54
Mamma Andersson 92
Manna, Jumana 106
map 30, 61, 62, 64, 88, 92, 106
Marclay, Christian 75
marker 74, 104, 105
Markey, Erin 87
Marshall, Kerry James 92
Martin, Agnes 87
Martin, Justin Lee 64, 92
mass media 10–12
master copy 5, 6, 46–50, 107, 108
Matisse, Henri 86
Matrix, The 25
Mazzanti, Enrico *17, 18*
McArthur, Park 106

McGee, Barry 104
McIntosh, Peggy 35
McLaren, Norman 106
McQueen, Steve 13
mechanical 2, 89
media 1, 9, 13, 14, 23, 31, 33, 46, 47, 49, 50, 60–63, 65, 73, 83, 86, 89, 101, 105; alternative 47, 50; drawing media 39, 40, 47, 50, 64, 66; mixed media 39, 64, 104; traditional 39, 50, 64, 104
Meires, Cildo 11
memories 20, 30, 77, 99, 105
Memphis Milano 86
Mendieta, Ana 90
Mengfu, Zhao 78
Meow Wolf 94
Mesfin, Gelila 83
Mickey Mouse 15
Minimalism 2
Minnick, Alyssa 56
Modern Inventions 17, 18
Modern Times 17, 18
Monet 42
monochromatic 2, 62
Monogram 10
Mono-ha 106
Montgomery, Guen 6, 93
Moon, Sanghyuk 104
More Love Hours Than Can Ever Be Repaid and The Wages of Sin 12
Morgan, Jenny 105
mortality 30
Moscheta, Marcelo 93
movement 8–11, 64, 67, 84, 92
Moyer-Battick, Milo 80
Mueller, Ellen 38
museum 3, 20, 27, 32, 78, 103
music 8, 9, 11, 12, 16, 32, 66, 76
Mutu, Wangechi 87, 88

Native American 7
natural 2, 8, 78, 81, 99
nature 2, 30, 46, 89, 96, 102
Needs More Chicken 27
Neel, Alice 81
negative space 2
Negativland 11
Nelson, Maggie 82
New Portraits 13, 24

New York Close Up 33
news 20, 30, 31
nonrepresentational 39
Nova Trilogy, The 10

O'Connor, Meghan 95
O'Neil, Dan 15
O'Neil, Robyn 40
Obama, Michelle 83
observational drawing 61, 95, 102
oil paint 80, 104, 105
Oldham, Julia 60, 97
Ondak, Roman 82
Oppenheim, Dennis 15
organizational 30
Over the Rainbow 16
Owens, Fred 92

Parker, Cornelia 103
Patrick, Mitch 100
pattern 67, 78, 86
PBS 33
performance 9, 47, 50, 82, 86, 87, 90, 91, 106
Pet Store, The 17
Peto, John 101
Pettibon, Raymond 76
Peyton, Elizabeth 81
Pfleumer, Fritz 9
Phillips, Bertram 17
philosophy 30, 41
photography 9, 11, 60, 73, 75, 87–89, 98, 101, 102
photomontage 9
physical 2, 20, 35, 57, 67, 71, 75, 78, 92, 93, 95, 100, 105
Picasso, Pablo 2, 8, 81
Pieter Bruegel the Elder 76
Pinocchio 17, 18
place 8, 30, 39, 40, 60, 61, 77, 106
play 1, 3, 59, 64–68, 70, 89, 91–94
poetry 9, 91, 102
point of view 32
politics 10, 30, 33
Polk, Andy 96
Polke, Sigmar 10, 92
Pontormo 75
Pop Art 2, 10, 104
popcorn 61
pose 60

power 1, 7, 8, 23, 30, 41, 81, 88
precise 44, 66, 79
pressure 65, 95
Prince of Wales (Midpul) 81
Prince, Richard 13
principles of design *see* elements and principles of design
print-on-demand 62
privilege 7, 30, 34, 35, 37, 58, 106, 108; age 14, 34, 42; class 14, 34, 35, 42; gender identity 7, 14, 34, 35, 42, 94; political affiliation 14, 35, 42; race 7, 14, 34, 35, 42; religion 14, 34, 35, 42; sexual identity 14, 42
profit 7, 15, 16, 19, 24, 27
proportions 60
Psycho 12
public domain 15, 16, 25, 98
Public Enemy 12, 76
Puff the Magic Dragon 16

Queen and Country 13
Queen Bey *see* Beyoncé
quietly 77

Rama, Carol 82
Rankin/Bass Christmas specials 17
rap 12
Rapper's Delight 11
Rauch, Neo 92
Rauschenberg, Robert 10, 25, 75, 103, 104
readymade 9
red 41
RedBubble 62
reflection 3, 25, 34, 36, 70, 72
relationship 23, 30, 47, 74, 75, 88, 89, 101, 102
remix 6, 8, 9, 26, 28, 74, 76, 79, 82, 83, 86–90, 94, 99, 100, 102, 103
Ren & Stimpy Show 17
repetition 2, 65, 87, 102, 106
repetitious 2
repetitive 66, 67, 98, 106
rhythm 79
Richter, Gerhard 10
RIP! A Remix Manifesto 28
ritual 59
Rivers, Larry 104, 105

Robbins, Cameron 93
Rocklyn, Ry 77
Rosler, Martha 88
Ross, Amy 98
Rudolph 17
Ryals, Katherine 100

sampling 6, 12, 25, 75, 76
scale 13, 50, 61–63, 65, 86, 97
Schaeffer, Pierre 9
Schoedsak, Ernest B. *17*
Schwitters, Kurt 9, 103
science 15, 30, 100, 101
science fiction 86, 99, 100
Scudder, Jefferey Alan 80
sculpture 9, 24, 31, 33, 73, 80, 81, 87, 100, 104
scumbling 65
self-portrait 60, 91, 98
senses 30, 35–37, 39, 58, 71, 72
sewing 105
ShareAlike 26
Shields, Alan 86
Shorr, Collier 83
Shrigley, David 81
sight 35, 93
silhouettes 86
Simpson, Buster 93
Simpsons, The 17
Situationism 10, 11
size 33, 81, 87
sketchbook 31–33, 39, 48, 58, 65, 70, 74, 75, 78, 80, 85, 86
Skoglund, Sandy 88
Skyers, Evellin 48
smell 14, 35, 36, 39, 40, 93
Smith, Kiki 81, 86
Smith, Philip 11
Snow White 17, 18
social justice 30
Society of the Spectacle 10
Society6 62
soft 78
Soft Machine, The 10
Sokolow, Deb 103
Sommer, Charles 1, 99
Sony 11
sound 9, 11, 14, 35, 39
South Africa 41
South Park 17

speed 65, 78
Spero, Nancy 81
spirituality 30
Springfield, Molly 1, 92, 100
Stalenhag, Simon 99
Steal This Film 28
Steamboat Bill 17
Steamboat Willie 17
Stewart, Ian 31, 103
Still Life with Chair Caning 8
stippling 65
Stockholder, Jessica 92
Stranger in the Village 12
string 50, 66
strong 30, 35, 94
Stuart, Michelle 106
subject 1, 8, 14, 31, 32, 36, 39, 41, 44, 47, 48, 61, 63, 68, 71–73, 95
Sugarhill Gang 11
Sulpy, Alessandra 64, 104
Sunstrum, Pamela Phatsimo 92
systems 10, 11, 19, 26, 30, 61, 80, 91
Sze, Sarah 74

Taaffe, Phillip 86
taste 14, 35, 36, 39
Tavern, Amy 65, 105
Teaching Notes 33
technical 47
technology 6, 9, 30, 35, 100
Tenniel, John *17, 18*
the everyday 30, 82, 84, 103
Thek, Paul 33, 106, 108
thumbnails 36, 68, 69, 95
tight 2, 99, 100
Tjapaltjarri, Warlimpirrnga 81
Tjapanangka, Tjumpo 81
Tomaselli, Fred 86
touch 35, 39, 75, 84
tour 32
travel 30, 31, 77, 78, 81
Treviño, René 92
triangle 70, 71
Triumph of the Nerds 15

Tuttle, Richard 93
Tuymans, Luc 92
Twombly, Cy 81, 87
Tzara, Tristan 9

Untitled (At Jennie Richee, they admire the beauty of the tropical nimbus clouds) 10

value 6, 16, 46, 61, 84, 97, 102
Van Beuren Studios 76
Van Hamersveld, John 25
Vasnetsov, Yuri 98
VCR 11
Velozo, Alex 80
vinyl records 9
Vostell, Wolf 10

walk 33
Walker, Kara 34, 75, 81, 92, 106
Warhol, Andy 10, 25, 104
wax cylinders 9
weather 30, 31, 80
Weiner, Lawrence 82, 101
Weiss, Jessica 79
Wesselman, Tom 105
West, Kanye 12, 75
what if 69
White Privilege: Unpacking the Invisible Knapsack 35
Williams, Sue 75
Wilson, Fred 103
Witkin, Jerome 105
World War I 9
World War II 10
Wu Tang Clan 76

xerography 10, 11
Xerox 914 (copier) 10
Xerox Alto (copier) *see* xerography

Yes Men, The 12
Yo! Bum Rush the Show 12

Zazzle 62